Francis William Pitt Greenwood

Lives of the Twelve Apostles

Francis William Pitt Greenwood

Lives of the Twelve Apostles

ISBN/EAN: 9783337333850

Printed in Europe, USA, Canada, Australia, Japan

Cover: Foto ©Lupo / pixelio.de

More available books at **www.hansebooks.com**

LIVES

OF

THE TWELVE APOSTLES,

TO WHICH IS PREFIXED

A LIFE OF

JOHN THE BAPTIST.

BY

F. W. P. GREENWOOD.

[Republished from the Third Edition by request of the "Ladies' Commission on Sunday-School Books."]

BOSTON:
AMERICAN UNITARIAN ASSOCIATION.
1874.

PREFACE

TO THE SECOND EDITION.

THE present edition of the "Lives of the Twelve Apostles" will, it is hoped, be found an improvement on the first. The work has been considerably enlarged, and its form has, in some respects, been changed. A Life of John the Baptist is now prefixed to the other lives, and a Life of the Apostle Matthias is added at the close. The Notes, which, in the first edition, were printed at the end of the volume, have either been incorporated with the text, or printed in their several places as foot-notes. Authorities have been reconsulted, and critical conclusions reconsidered.

It has been suggested to the author, from more than one respected source, that lives of Saint Paul, and of the Evangelists Mark and Luke, would be a desirable addition to the biographies of the Apostolic Twelve. ' But he has been fearful of injuring thereby the unity of his group,— that group which immediately surrounded our Lord, and whose lives are connected with his in the Gospel accounts; and he has therefore thought it more advisable to limit himself to the insertion of a life of the great Forerunner, which properly precedes the other histories.

In the Notes to the first edition, the author had named the days on which the Apostles are severally commemorated in the Western Church, and had also given the Collects, or short, comprehensive prayers, which are appropriated to those days in the Liturgy of the Church of England. To those Collects he has now subjoined some pieces of selected poetry, chiefly from late works of Bishop Mant and of Keble, with a view of increasing the religious impression of the volume, and adding somewhat of a devotional to its scriptural and biographical character. They who do not attach any peculiar sacredness to the days which are set apart to the Apostles and Saints by some churches may yet have their affections profitably engaged, at any convenient periods, by a devotional application of those lives and examples which have been bequeathed to the Church universal.

The same sentiments of affection, respect, and duty which prompted the author to dedicate the first edition of these "Lives" to "THE MEMBERS OF THE SOCIETY WORSHIPPING AT KING'S CHAPEL" induce him to inscribe the volume in its present form to the same friends, with the hope that it may prove more deserving than before of their acceptance and approbation.

FRANCIS W. P. GREENWOOD.

October 4, 1835.

CONTENTS.

	PAGE
LIFE OF JOHN THE BAPTIST	1
LIVES OF THE APOSTLES.— THE TWELVE	27
SIMON PETER	39
ANDREW	73
JAMES THE GREATER	79
JOHN	91
PHILIP	109
BARTHOLOMEW	114
THOMAS	120
MATTHEW	135
JAMES THE LESS	146
JUDE	158
SIMON ZELOTES	163
JUDAS ISCARIOT	165
MATTHIAS	184
CONCLUDING REMARKS	188

COLLECTS AND HYMNS.

The order of names which follows differs from that of the above list, and is the order in which the days occur in the calendar.

Saint Andrew's day, November 30	203
Saint Thomas's day, December 21	205

Saint John the Evangelist's day, December 27 207
Saint Matthias's day, February 24 210
Saint Philip and Saint James's day, May 1 212
Saint John the Baptist's Day, June 24 214
Saint Peter's day, June 29 216
Saint James's day, July 26 221
Saint Bartholomew's day, August 24 223
Saint Matthew's day, September 21 225
Saint Simon and Saint Jude's day, October 28 230

LIFE

OF

JOHN THE BAPTIST.

As John the Baptist presented himself to his countrymen as the herald and precursor of Jesus, and was acknowledged by Jesus to be so, and as his history is remarkably connected with the early part of the history of our Lord, the notices which are given of him in the Scriptures possess unusual interest. It is my purpose to examine these notices in their order, so as to present, as far as the materials will permit, a continuous view of his life. This life will naturally precede the lives of those who were afterwards sent by the Messiah to publish his laws and doctrines, as John was sent from above to be his harbinger.

In the first chapter of Luke's Gospel, we have an account of the particulars attending the birth of the Baptist. His father was a priest by the name of Zacharias; and his mother, whose name was Elizabeth, " was of the daughters of Aaron "; so that he was by birth of the order of priesthood, and on the side of both father and mother, of sacerdotal descent. He was the child of their old age. His father Zacharias was, as is said by the Evangelist, " of the course of Abia." To understand this expression, we must recur to the fact, stated in the First Book of Chronicles, that David divided the descendants of Aaron into twenty-four orders, named after the chief men among them, who should attend to the service of the temple in rotation. The eighth of these orders, or courses, was that of Abijah, or Abia, and the one to which Zacharias belonged.

What was more honorable to the parents of John than their official and hereditary sanctity, they were really holy and virtuous people. " They were both righteous before God, walking in all the commandments and ordinances of the Lord, blameless." No parentage could be more fit for the forerunner of the holy Jesus.

As Zacharias was officiating in the temple in his turn, or "in the order of his course," an angel appeared to him, predicted the birth of his son, and declared that his name should be John, which means, in the Hebrew language, the gift or grace of God. He added that his birth would be the cause of rejoicing to many; that he would be "great in the sight of the Lord"; that he would be singularly abstemious, and "filled with the Holy Spirit"; and that he should go before the Lord "in the spirit and power of Elias." It was a general expectation among the Jews, that the prophet Elias, or Elijah, was to reappear on earth in person, to announce the arrival of the Messiah; and this expectation was founded on one or two passages of the Book of Malachi, such as, "Behold I will send my messenger, and he shall prepare the way before me"; and still more explicitly, "Behold I will send you Elijah the prophet before the coming of the great and dreadful day of the Lord." The words of the angel evidently refer to this prophecy, and at the same time imply that the messenger of the Lord, who was to precede and announce the Messiah, was not to be Elijah himself, according to common expectation, but one who should "go before him in the spirit and power of Elijah," — one who, like Elijah, should be endowed with a perception of God's purposes towards mankind, and with power to operate on their minds, to persuade them to repentance, and thus "to make ready a people prepared for the Lord."

In due time John was born; and his birth took place six months before that of Jesus, whose mother Mary was the cousin of his mother Elizabeth. As the former event may be considered the dawn which betokened the rising of the Sun of Righteousness, we perceive the propriety of its being recorded by Luke in the beginning of his Gospel. The circumcision of John took place, as was customary among the Jews, on the eighth day after his birth; and on this day his father Zacharias recovered the use of his speech, of which he had been deprived, as a sign of the truth of what the angel had told him. "He spake, and praised God"; and his joy burst forth in the words of that sublime and holy song, beginning, "Blessed be the Lord God of Israel, for he hath visited and redeemed his people." We are then told that "the child grew, and waxed strong in spirit, and was in the deserts till the day of his showing unto Israel." The meaning of this last clause is not that John, in his early childhood, lived alone in a wilderness, but that he passed his days, till he was called to the exercise of his mission, in the privacy of his parents' abode, which was in the deserts or hill-country of Judæa, as we are informed in the former part of the same chapter. As Hebron was the capital of this hill-country, and was, moreover, one of the cities appointed for the residence of the priests, it was probably the place where John passed his childhood with his parents, as Jesus did with his. Its distance south of Jerusalem was between twenty and thirty, and in the same direction from Nazareth about seventy miles.

Nothing more is related of John, till we hear of his call to commence his great work. The period of his entrance on his ministry is marked with great precision. "Now in the fifteenth year of the reign of Tiberius Cæsar, Pontius Pilate being governor of Judæa, and Herod being tetrarch of Galilee, and his brother Philip tetrarch of Iturea and of the region of Trachonitis, and Lysanias the tetrarch of Abilene, Annas and Caiaphas being the high-priests, the word of God came unto John the son of Zacharias, in the wilderness. And he came into all the country about Jordan, preaching the baptism of repentance for the remission of sins." The call came to him in the wilderness, or thinly peopled hill-country, where his family resided; and beginning there, he advanced towards Jerusalem, confining himself to the same retired portions of Judæa, and preaching to those who resorted to him in increasing numbers, till he reached Bethabara beyond Jordan, a few miles from the holy city, where he held his principal station. All this district of country bordered upon the sacred river Jordan, in which he baptized those who were affected by his preaching, and enlisted themselves among his disciples. Bethabara was probably near a fordable part of the river, as the meaning of the word is "the house of the passage." It was therefore a convenient place of resort for his hearers.

The great doctrine which the Baptist preached, as preparatory to the Redeemer's kingdom, was repentance. "In those days," says the account of Matthew, "came John the Baptist, preaching in the wilderness of Judæa, and saying, Repent ye; for the kingdom of heaven is at hand. For this is he that was spoken of by the prophet Esaias, saying, The voice of one crying in the wilderness, Prepare ye the way of the Lord, make his path straight." His custom, which was not a new one among the Jews, was to baptize those who believed his warnings, and joined themselves to him as converts or disciples, that he might signify the cleansing and renewing of mind which was necessary for the reception of the new state of things which was approaching, as well as essential to the repentance which he himself so earnestly insisted on. And the same meaning of moral preparation is to be attributed to the prophetic metaphors of filling the valleys and bringing low the mountains and hills, making the crooked ways straight, and the rough smooth, which were duties belonging to the herald and forerunner of the anointed Prince of peace.

The appearance and habits of living which were assumed and practised by John, while he was preaching and baptizing, and to which he had no doubt accustomed himself from tender age, were consistent with his character as the representative of Elijah. His clothing was coarse, and his food such as the deserts yielded. "And the same

JOHN THE BAPTIST.

John had his raiment of camel's hair, and a leathern girdle about his loins; and his meat was locusts and wild honey."* Compare this account of Matthew with the description given in the Second Book of Kings of Elijah. "What manner of man," inquired Ahaziah of his messengers, "was he who came up to meet you, and told you these words? And they answered him, He was an hairy man, and girt with a girdle of leather about his loins. And he said, It is Elijah the Tishbite." † This was probably a usual kind of dress with the ancient prophets, especially in times of distress or great excitement. The insect called the locust was allowed as food by the Levitical law, ‡ and travellers assure us that it is eaten in Eastern countries at the present day, and that the bees of Palestine still deposit their stores in the holes of the rocks in such abundance that the honey is sometimes seen flowing down the surface.

Living in this severe manner, and proclaiming on the wild banks of the Jordan the approach of the Messiah's reign and Israel's redemption, John drew universal regard, and the desert became populous around him. "Then went out to him Jerusalem and all Judæa, and all the region round about Jordan, and were baptized of him in Jordan, confessing their sins." § I have already

* Matt. iii. 4.   ‡ Lev. xi. 22.
† 2 Kings i. 8.   § Matt. iii. 5.

said that the ceremony of baptism, or washing with water, was not new among the Jews, as significant of change and renewal, on the reception of converts or disciples to proposed forms of faith or discipline. It may be added, that it was a current opinion among the Jews, founded as usual on prophecy, that the forerunner of the Messiah, or Messiah himself, or both, would use the form of baptism, when the time of Israel's redemption should come. A passage in Zechariah which was thought to warrant this opinion is at least poetically descriptive of the office of John at his station of Bethabara beyond Jordan. "In that day there shall be a fountain opened to the house of David and to the inhabitants of Jerusalem, for sin and for uncleanness." *

The character of John's preaching and instructions is set forth with a great degree of particularity in the account which is given by Luke of his exhortations and advice to various classes of persons, from which it plainly appears that his doctrine was of a direct and practical kind, and that the preparation which he inculcated was of a moral nature entirely. He warned the people not to rely with their wonted pride on their being the children of Abraham, but to "bring forth fruits worthy of repentance." He was surprised to see the Pharisees and Sadducees resorting to

* Zech. xiii. 1.

him; because they were so filled with this pride, and so confident in the merit of their ceremonial righteousness. He was surprised that they should come to his baptism, which was one of real and practical, not formal or mystical repentance. "O generation of vipers!" he exclaimed, "children of deceit and hypocrisy! who hath warned you to flee from the wrath to come?"

When "the people asked him, saying, What shall we do then?" he indicated by his answer what was the nature of those fruits which were worthy of repentance, those deeds which proved a true change of heart and mind;—he said unto them, "He that hath two coats, let him impart to him that hath none; and he that hath meat, let him do likewise." The great duty of benevolence is here enforced, and illustrated by one of its simple modes, and exalted in clear superiority above the works of the law.

And when the publicans, or tax-gatherers, came to be baptized, "and said unto him, Master, what shall we do? he said unto them, Exact no more than that which is appointed you." He knew their peculiar temptations, and their besetting sin, arising from the circumstances of their situation, and he therefore warned them against the spirit of extortion, and exhorted them to honesty, moderation, and mercy.

"And the soldiers likewise demanded of him,

saying, And what shall we do? And he said unto them, Do violence to no man, neither accuse any falsely; and be content with your wages."

This is all quite practical and plain, and shows that the eremitical Baptist, severe as he was in his manners, solitary in his haunts, and striking in his whole appearance and deportment, was yet simple and direct in his teaching, and did not affect to move in a cloud of mysticism. It denotes also, that though he may have had, on some points, mistaken views of the Messiah's kingdom, and did not embrace the whole extent of its spirituality, yet he was well aware that it was to be a moral reformation, without which there could be no national deliverance, and that all who would be its subjects and partake of its blessings could secure their place only by repentance and righteousness of life. This was one proof of the truth and divinity of his mission. Excited as the people were by the mere proclamation of the coming deliverer, he made no further use of the excitement than to direct it to moral ends. He knew that this was the limit of his commission. He said and did nothing to rouse the minds of his hearers to any hostile manifestations; but whether they were Pharisees, Sadducees, publicans, or soldiers, he only exhorted them to true repentance and the performance of the charitable and peaceful duties. Here also we may observe a remarkable, and I may say a miraculous, conformity between the spirit of the Baptist's preaching and the spirit of the Messiah's religion as it was afterwards developed. There is no appearance of any intimacy or collusion between them. They lived seventy miles apart from each other, — the one in Nazareth of Galilee, and the other in Hebron of Judæa, — and therefore, though related to each other, had probably met but seldom, up to the time of the public appearance of John as a preacher and prophet. There is evidently an unprepared and undesigned agreement between the introduction and the perfection of the new dispensation; a spiritual agreement which could not have existed between two uninspired Jews, nurtured in the prejudices and traditions of their nation. The true light was preceded by the true witness. The dawning was a pure and correct, though faint, likeness of the day.

Distinguished, however, as John the Baptist had become by his austere mode of life, by his prophetic dress and bearing, by his bold, earnest, and authoritative teaching, by the crowds who appeared as his baptized disciples, and by his annunciation of the ardently longed-for Messiah, the people began to suppose that he might be the Messiah himself. If John had been only playing a part, and been under the influence of a worldly ambition, he might easily have turned this idea to his own advantage and personal exaltation. But he maintained his own proper place and duty, humbly and strictly. "And as the people were in expectation, and all men mused in their hearts of John, whether he were the Christ or not, John answered, saying unto them all, I indeed baptize you with water; but one mightier than I cometh, the latchet of whose shoes I am not worthy to unloose; he shall baptize you with the Holy Ghost and with fire."* John allowed that he performed the office of baptism as a teacher and reformer, but declared that it was only introductory and emblematic, only a baptism with water; while he who was soon to be manifested, the real Christ, to be whose servant he was himself unworthy, would baptize with a far more thorough, searching, and efficacious baptism, with a spiritual and purifying baptism, with the Holy Ghost and with fire. In using this latter expression, he perhaps had in his mind the passage of Malachi, which says, "And he shall sit as a refiner and purifier of silver; and he shall purify the sons of Levi, and purge them as gold and silver, that they may offer unto the Lord an offering in righteousness." John, however, changes the metaphor, and represents the Messiah as a husbandman, with his winnowing fan in his hand, thoroughly separating the wheat on his floor from

* Luke iii. 15.

the chaff, gathering the former into his granary, and burning the latter with fire.

And now the time arrives when he who was to come appears. "Then cometh Jesus from Galilee to Jordan, unto John, to be baptized of him." From the retirement of distant Galilee, where he had passed his youth in study and labor, and in docile subservience to his parents, Jesus, having entered upon his thirtieth year, which was the age of induction into the priestly office among the Jews,* travelled to Bethabara, and presented himself to his relative to be baptized. How eventful was this meeting between the son of Elizabeth and the son of Mary! They whose births had been announced by the angel Gabriel, and who had since lived apart in holy seclusion and quiet duty for thirty years, were now brought together by the call of God in the presence of assembled multitudes, and this was the first public interview between the commissioned herald and the anointed prince, between the messenger and the Redeemer. When John heard the request of Jesus to be baptized, he at first forbade, or refused him; for though he was not yet certified of his being the Christ, yet he was probably acquainted with the wonders attending his birth, and with his life of entire purity and holiness. Therefore he meekly remonstrated, "I

---

* Numbers iv.

have need to be baptized of thee, and comest thou to me?" But Jesus, who would commence his ministry with a public and solemn ordinance, and regardful, perhaps, of the usage by which the sons of Aaron were washed with water before they commenced the functions of the priesthood,* answered, "Suffer it to be so now; for thus it becometh us to fulfil all righteousness." Thus urged, or, it may be, commanded, John could no longer hesitate, and the two moved down through the silent crowd into the expectant stream, and its waters, more consecrated than consecrating, were poured on the Saviour's head.

> "Old Jordan smiled, receiving such high pay
>   For those small pains obedient he had spent,
> Making his waters guard the driéd way
>   Through wonders when to Canaan Israel went;
> Nor does he envy now Pactolus' streams,
> Or Eastern floods, whose paths are paved with gems." †

As Jesus came up from the river, the heavens were opened to declare his mission to the earth, the spirit of God descended with a dove-like motion upon him, and a voice was heard pronouncing, "This is my beloved Son, in whom I am well pleased." From this moment the ministry of Jesus commenced, and, "being full of the Holy Ghost, he returned from Jordan, and was led by the Spirit into the wilderness," ‡ where he fasted and was tempted.

* Exodus xxix. 4.   † Joseph Beaumont.   ‡ Luke iv. 1.

As we know that Jesus was thirty years of age when he began his ministry, and that this was the age prescribed by the Jewish law as the proper time for the commencement of sacred functions, it is probable that John began his ministry at the same age, and, being six months older than Jesus, we may draw the conclusion that he had been six months preaching and baptizing, when that manifestation of the Messiah took place which was the great end of his baptism.

At the expiration of our Saviour's sojourn in the wilderness, he returned to Bethabara, and took up his abode in that neighborhood. About the same time, the great council of the Jews, moved by the celebrity of John, and the surmises of the people concerning him, and being yet ignorant of the appearance and claims of Jesus, sent a formal deputation to the Baptist, to ascertain what he was, or assumed to be. "And this," says the Evangelist John,* "is the record," or rather the testimony, or free profession, "of John, when the Jews sent priests and Levites from Jerusalem to ask him, Who art thou? And he confessed, and denied not; but confessed, I am not the Christ." With decided and earnest reiteration he refused the kingly title. "And they asked him, What then? Art thou Elias?

* John i. 19.

And he saith, I am not." Though he did come in the spirit and power of Elijah, yet as he was aware that they intended to inquire whether he was Elijah himself, according to their notions, restored to earth to precede the Messiah, he was too honest to reply except in the negative. They pursued their interrogatories. "Art thou that prophet?" They asked him, in the pertinacity of their opinion that some one or another of the ancient prophets was to reappear in person, whether he was such a prophet. And he still answered, "No." Then, having exhausted their suppositions, and unwilling to go back to Jerusalem without some satisfactory answer, they said unto him, "Who art thou? that we may give an answer to them that sent us. What sayest thou of thyself?" The look of the Baptist, the humble and yet rapt and holy expression of his countenance, may be imagined, but not described, with which he said, in the sublime words of Isaiah, and standing in that forest by the flowing waters of Jordan, "I am the voice of one crying in the wilderness, Make straight the way of the Lord." It was immaterial what he was in person, or in name; he was only a voice, — a voice in the wilderness, — but yet a voice proclaiming to the world, and proclaiming truly and solemnly, "Make straight the way of the Lord."

As John had denied being either of the persons suggested, the deputation asked, in surprise, and perhaps with anger, why then he undertook to perform the important office of baptism. In answer, John declared, as he had before, that his baptism was but outward and introductory, whereas his successor and superior would baptize with a holier and mightier baptism. He intimated, moreover, that this exalted personage, though they knew him not, was even then among them. And thus he publicly declared to this official deputation the actual arrival of the Messiah.

The next day John saw Jesus coming toward him, and made him known to the people who were then assembled, by that memorable exclamation, "Behold the Lamb of God, which taketh away the sin of the world!"* He then went on to say, that this was he who, coming after him, was yet before him; that he did not at first know that he was the expected Redeemer, but that it was to make him manifest to Israel that he himself had come baptizing with water; and that on the day when he baptized him, he saw and heard those heavenly signs which convinced him that he was the Christ, for they were signs which he had been taught to look for. "He that sent me to baptize with water," said he, "the same said unto me, Upon whom thou shalt see

* John i. 29.

B

the Spirit descending, and remaining on him, the same is he who baptizeth with the Holy Ghost." * He then adds, "And I saw, and bare record, that this is the Son of God."

Again the next day after, as he was standing with two of his disciples, he looked on Jesus as he walked by, and said, "Behold the Lamb of God!" One of these disciples was Andrew, and the other probably was John the Evangelist; † and these two disciples of the forerunner of Christ were among the first disciples of Christ himself.

As Jesus was now manifested to Israel, and had begun his work, the ministry of John may be said to have closed. Still, however, he co-operated as he was able with his Master, and continued to baptize. Jesus also, or rather his disciples, began to baptize in Judæa; and this seems to have excited the jealousy of the disciples of John, who came and reported it to him.‡ The Baptist at this time had moved higher up the river, and "was baptizing in Enon, near to Salim, because there was much water there." His reply to his disciples hushed their murmurings, and was another humble, affectionate, and

---

* John i. 33.

† When John speaks of a disciple, without mentioning his name, he is supposed to intend himself.

‡ John iii. 22; iv. 2.

manly testimony to the superior dignity of Jesus. He told them, that they themselves would bear him witness, that he said he was not the Christ, but was sent before him. He declared that as the friend of the bridegroom rejoiced to hear the bridegroom's voice, so his joy was fulfilled. He added those affecting and prophetic words, "He must increase, but I must decrease." He then spoke at large of the divine truth and glory of the mission of Christ, concluding, "He that believeth on the Son hath everlasting life; and he that believeth not the Son shall not see life; but the wrath of God abideth on him."

"He must increase, but I must decrease." Perhaps John did not himself know how soon and how fearfully those words were to be fulfilled. He could not have known it; because, though content to occupy an inferior station, he yet looked for some signal and outward display of the Messiah's kingdom, to be manifested, however, with accompanying holiness, in which he might participate, or at least rejoice. But this was not to be granted him. His work and his life were soon to be ended.

The popularity of John had attracted the notice of Herod the tetrarch, surnamed Antipas, who was the son of that Herod who had thirty years ago commanded the slaughter of the infants of Bethlehem. He had sent for the Baptist, and conversed with him; not that he was desirous of hearing truth, but he was anxious to see so celebrated a person; and celebrity was, in his eyes, as it is in the eyes of many, the great thing, whether it appertain to a buffoon or a saint. But John reproved him for his marriage with Herodias, his brother Philip's wife, which so incensed that bad woman, that she caused her infatuated husband to throw him into prison; which prison, according to the historian Josephus, was the fortress of Machærus, on the northern border of the Dead Sea. Here John was doomed to lie inactive, — another proof of the proverbial fickleness of the favor of great men and princes, — but still retaining the respect of Herod on account of his integrity and wisdom, and causing him to fear on account of his favor with the people. Herodias would have killed him at first; "but she could not; for Herod feared John, knowing that he was a just man and an holy, and observed him." But she was revengeful as she was licentious, and she did not forget the Baptist's offence, nor her own deadly purpose.

While John was lying thus in prison, in the power of a weak prince, who was under the influence of a wicked and dangerous woman, he heard of the works of Christ, but heard nothing which promised deliverance. Either suffering himself to become impatient, at which we need not wonder, or desiring to obtain the most definite information regarding the proceedings and designs of Jesus, he sent unto him two of his disciples, who adhered to him in all his troubles, to inquire of him, "Art thou he that should come, or do we look for another?" The answer which Jesus returned, while it reminded him of the continued testimonials of the Spirit to his mission by miracles, directed him to the spiritual nature of his kingdom, which was evinced by his preaching its glad tidings to the poor. And this answer probably calmed the troubled though strong mind of John, and satisfied him that he must now look for deliverance to that kingdom alone, " where the wicked cease from troubling, and the weary are at rest."

As the messengers of John departed, Jesus began to speak concerning him to the surrounding multitude, and rendered a testimony to his prophetic mission, which proves his own unshaken confidence in the Baptist's integrity. What, he asked them, did they go out into the deserts of Judæa to see? Not surely the wind-shaken reeds on the banks of the Jordan; not a man clothed in fine and costly raiment, for men thus clothed were to be found in palaces, not deserts; but they went for the purpose of seeing a prophet. And he was indeed more than a common prophet. He had more than a common mission, and he had faithfully discharged it. He was sent to prepare the way of the Messiah, and he had prepared it. Of those who had hitherto been raised up for important purposes by the Almighty, none had been greater than John the Baptist; and yet even he entertained so inadequate notions of the entire spirituality of the Messiah's kingdom, that the least among those who should truly receive it, in its pure separateness from the world, would be greater than he.

After bearing this open testimony to the truth of John's divine mission, and the reality of his prophetic character,—a truth and reality which were not impaired by the imperfection of his views,—Jesus closes the discourse by some remarks on the effect of his ministry in connection with his own. He speaks of the small number of those who had been moved to repentance by John the Baptist or by himself, and rebukes the people of that age for their perversity in rejecting both, although they were so different from each other in character and habits. John, being of an austere and retired deportment, was charged with being melancholy or crazed; — they said, "He hath a devil." He himself, mingling more freely with men of all ranks, and partaking of their entertainments, was rudely accused of being "a gluttonous man and a wine-bibber, a friend of publicans and sinners." Such a stubborn and petulant generation might be fitly likened to children in the streets, who would refuse to join with their companions in any games, and would neither dance to their festive piping, nor lament with them when they imitated the funeral wail.

It was probably about three months after this occurrence that the revengeful Herodias found an opportunity of accomplishing the destruction of the Baptist. As Herod was keeping his birthday, by a magnificent supper which he gave to his lords and captains, she sent her daughter by her former husband * into the hall, to dance before him and his guests. The exhibition pleased the tetrarch to such a degree, that he promised with an oath to grant the daughter whatsoever she should ask, even to the half of his kingdom. The young dancer went out, and reported this to her mother, and consulted her with regard to the request which she should prefer. Herodias, without hesitation, and feeling that the dark game was now in her own cruel hands, told her daughter to ask for the head of John the Baptist; and, in order to make sure of her prey, and guard against any humane deception, she added the condition, that the head should be brought to her on a "charger," or large dish. For such a terrible request the sobered king was wholly unprepared,

* She had a daughter, as Josephus tells us, by the name of Salome.

and he was "exceeding sorry." Nevertheless, he conceived himself bound by his oath, — as if an oath could bind the soul to crime, — and sent an executioner to the prison to do the wicked deed. "It was the holy purpose of God," says Bishop Hall, "that he who had baptized with water should now be baptized with blood." The blameless John, — the preacher of repentance and righteousness, — the holy reprover of vice, whether a publican's or a king's, — was beheaded in the prison. "For one minute's pain, he is possessed of endless joy; and as he came before his Saviour into the world, so is he gone before him into heaven." His faithful disciples forsook him not, though dead, but came, and "took up the body and buried it"; and then went and informed Jesus of what had taken place.

The uneasy conscience of Herod Antipas would not suffer him to forget the image of his victim. When he afterwards heard of the fame of Jesus, he expressed his belief that it was John the Baptist, whom he had beheaded, risen from the dead.

It is not told us in the Gospels where the Baptist was buried by his disciples. Less authentic accounts state, that "in the time of Julian the apostate, his tomb was shown at Samaria, where the inhabitants opened it, and burnt part of his bones; while the rest were saved by some Christians, who carried them to an abbot of Jerusalem, named Philip." *

The Roman Church celebrates the martyrdom of John the Baptist on the 29th of August. But the day on which he is especially commemorated is the 24th of June, which is kept as the day of his nativity; it being the only nativity, besides that of our Saviour, which that church observes. The Apostles and other saints bore witness to the truth more especially by their deaths, but John more especially by his birth, with its concomitants. A kind of perpetual commentary is thus afforded on the declaration of the angel, that "many shall rejoice in his birth." And as our Lord's nativity is observed on the 25th of December, and he was about six months younger than John, the 24th of June is properly selected as the birthday of the latter. Here again a comment of the same poetical character, on another text, has sometimes been noticed. The days, which begin to lengthen at the first of those dates, and to grow shorter at the last, point to that saying of the Baptist already quoted, "He must increase, but I must decrease."

But leaving these somewhat fanciful allusions, we cannot fail to observe that the life of the Baptist, setting forth so clearly and prominently the gravity, disinterestedness, courage, and purity of

* Calmet.

his character, is a worthy introduction to the Lives of that "glorious company of the Apostles," who praised God as he did in life and death, who surround the Lamb in heaven as they did on earth, and whose example enforces that of the forerunner, which so earnestly exhorts us to "constantly speak the truth, boldly rebuke vice, and patiently suffer for the truth's sake." O for more of that primitive faith and virtue! for more witnesses, more disciples!

> "Where is the lore the Baptist taught,
>   The soul unswerving, and the fearless tongue ?
> The much-enduring wisdom, sought
>   By lonely prayer the haunted rocks among ?
>   Who counts it gain
>   His light should wane,
> So the whole world to Jesus throng ?"

LIVES OF THE APOSTLES.

THE TWELVE.

JESUS CHRIST, the Saviour and Teacher sent from God, soon after he commenced his ministry, selected twelve men to be his immediate followers and confidential disciples. "Now the names of the twelve Apostles are these: the first, SIMON who is called PETER, and ANDREW his brother; JAMES the son of ZEBEDEE, and JOHN his brother; PHILIP, and BARTHOLOMEW; THOMAS, and MATTHEW the publican; JAMES the son of ALPHEUS, and LEBBEUS, whose surname was THADDEUS; SIMON the Canaanite, and JUDAS ISCARIOT, who also betrayed him." This list of the Apostles is taken from the Gospel of Matthew, who was himself one of them. We are also presented with a similar catalogue in the Gospels of Mark and Luke, and in the Book of Acts.*

---

* Matthew's list is from chap. x, 2, 3, 4. For facility of reference, the three remaining lists of the twelve are here subjoined.
"And Simon he surnamed Peter; and James the son of Zebe-

Why the exact number of twelve was appointed, it is more difficult than important to determine. Perhaps it was done in compliance with the attachment of the Jews to that number. Perhaps it was with a more particular reference to the number of the sons of Jacob, and the tribes of which they were the progenitors and founders; "Ye also," says Jesus, "shall sit upon twelve thrones, judging the twelve tribes of Israel." Under the new dispensation, ye twelve, whom I have chosen, shall exercise the same spiritual authority and rule as did the twelve patriarchs under the old dispensation. Ye shall be regarded with the same religious respect. Ye shall give laws and ordinances to my people.

The motives which induced the Master to call to himself a select company of disciples seem to

---

dee; and John the brother of James; and he surnamed them Boanerges, which is, The Sons of Thunder; and Andrew; and Philip; and Bartholomew; and Matthew; and Thomas; and James the son of Alpheus; and Thaddeus; and Simon the Canaanite; and Judas Iscariot, who also betrayed him." *Mark* iii. 16, 17, 18, 19.

"Simon, whom he also named Peter; and Andrew his brother; James and John; Philip and Bartholomew; Matthew and Thomas; James the son of Alpheus, and Simon called Zelotes; and Judas the brother of James, and Judas Iscariot, who also was the traitor." *Luke* vi. 14, 15, 16.

"Peter and James and John and Andrew, Philip and Thomas, Bartholomew and Matthew, James the son of Alpheus, and Simon Zelotes, and Judas the brother of James." *Acts* i. 13.

be more obvious. It was proper and even necessary that he should have some followers in whom he might particularly confide, and who should be always near him and about him.

It was needful, in the first place, that he should be thus attended, in order that the wonders which he worked in confirmation of the divinity of his mission should be nearly inspected and credibly attested. I deem it one of the strongest evidences of the truth of our Saviour's miracles, that they were performed, not only in sight of the multitude, but of a select company, who were too familiar with him to be deceived themselves, and too honest to join with him in deceiving others. Being brought into the midst of his operations, they were qualified to judge of their reality and integrity, and therefore qualified to report them to the world with all the warmth of conviction, and all the directness, particularity, and authority of constant experience and repeated vision. A changing crowd, never composed perhaps on any two occasions of the same materials, might have been mistaken; but a band of twelve companions could not have been. They were fitted, as in no other way they could have been so well, for the purpose of declaring to men the power from above with which their Master was invested; and that they might be thus prepared was one of his designs in choosing them. "Ye are *witnesses* of these things," said he to the eleven, after his resurrection from the dead. He evinced a consciousness of innocence and sincerity by admitting so many partakers of his secret counsels and his daily deeds; and he manifested his wisdom by securing such an irrefragable testimony to the reality of those signs from Heaven which pointed him out as truly the Son of God.

The apostles were selected, in the second place, in order that, by reiterated instruction, they might become well acquainted with the religion which their Master was about to establish on the earth. "It is given unto you to know the mysteries of the kingdom of heaven." Jesus addressed himself to all who had ears to hear, but more particularly to those twelve who were to preach in his name when he should be lifted up; because, through them, mankind were to receive the tidings of his salvation. He chose them, that he might teach them, so that they in turn might teach. His doctrine was so new, so different from what men had been used to dignify with the title of religion, that occasional lessons to the multitude, uttered in a confined sphere and by a single individual, would hardly have served the purpose of rendering it familiar and making it well understood. On this account it was more minutely, clearly, and repeatedly explained to a select class of pupils, who were thus prepared to become instructors themselves, and, by penetrating into different and distant countries, to disseminate among the nations of the earth a religious system which was at first promulgated to the Jewish people, and limited to their small inheritance alone. They were called *apostles*, because they were *sent* out into the world.* Before they were sent, they were instructed in the purposes and powers of their mission. And how slow they were to comprehend, after all the pains which had been bestowed on them, the true nature of the Messiah's kingdom and laws, may be read in their own confessions of ignorance. It was late, and not till after supernatural illumination, that they were thoroughly initiated in the true meaning of the religion which they were commissioned to preach and to spread. This is a fact which forcibly attests, not the dulness of the disciples, for their natural perceptions were as quick as those of other men, but the need there was of their being well grounded in the doctrines of Christ, and the opposition which existed between the entire simplicity and spirituality of those doctrines and the grossness of their own expectations and of the common opinions of the world.

It may be well to add to the above reasons for the separation of the twelve, that they were brought into a close personal intimacy with the Saviour, in

---

* From the Greek αποστελλω (*apostello*), "I send."

order that they might study his example, borrow his spirit, and so receive the image of his life that they might reflect it in their own. They were both the witnesses and the objects and recipients of that divine gentleness, compassion, and benevolence, which from that fountain flowed out all abroad on everything. They could not be so much in his society without being affected by the bland influences of his manners and character. It was very probably intended that they should be thus affected; that they should behold the temper of Christianity in a living form; its doctrines set forth in conduct; its precepts illustrated by a perpetually corresponding practice; and that, beholding this, they should be touched by its beauty, and conformed in some measure to its likeness, and enabled to hold up, not only the description, but the copy of it, before the sight of men. It was almost an inevitable result of their situation, that they should imbibe a portion of the divine life of Christianity from their strict fellowship with its founder. Like those flowers which are known to drink in the light of the sun while he remains above the horizon, and then to give it out in mild flashes when the evening shades come on, so the disciples, while their Master sojourned with them, while the Sun of Righteousness shone upon them, absorbed the beaming excellence of his character, and then, when he left the earth, emitted it partially again amidst the moral darkness which surrounded them.

One other purpose, which the connection of the twelve disciples with our Saviour was fitted to answer, was, the qualification which it conferred on them for recording his deeds and words, and preserving to posterity the invaluable memorial. I know not how we, of this age, could have trusted implicitly to accounts of the origin and true principles of the Christian religion, which tradition alone might have brought down to us; nor is it easily conceivable how any persons could have been better prepared to render an authentic, trustworthy, and interesting history of our faith, than were those who accompanied Jesus through the several scenes of his ministry, and immediately succeeded him in publishing the Gospel. Accordingly, we find that two out of the four relations of our Saviour's life and death were written by two of the twelve disciples; and that the greater part of the remaining books of the New Testament were likewise composed by the original apostles, and by that distinguished individual whose apostleship was bestowed on him directly and miraculously from Heaven. It is true, that we are obliged to learn from tradition who the writers were of several of the sacred books; but a few facts of this simple nature might securely be trusted to its keeping, though at the same time it would be an improper depository and an unsafe vehicle for the numerous occurrences, sentiments, and precepts which constitute the Christian system. It is a self-evident proposition, that the chosen companions of Jesus, having witnessed his miracles, having been instructed in his religion, and made intimately acquainted with his character, were qualified in the best manner to convert their experience into history, and to transmit to the latest ages an indubitable standard of Christian truth.

Such appear to be our Saviour's motives, as far as we are authorized to judge of them, in nominating his twelve disciples. It becomes a matter of no inconsiderable interest to us to know something of the history, to ascertain something of the character, of those who were so peculiarly and so highly distinguished.

Who were those, in the first place, whom the Saviour of men, the Prince of Peace, the Son of God, chose out of the whole world, to be his companions, his friends, his pupils, his witnesses, his historians, his apostles? What were their qualities? How were they recommended to the notice of Jesus? What were their occupations, their condition, education, principles? It was a remarkable station which they were called upon to hold, — so near the person, so high in the confidence, of the most exalted being who ever appeared on our earth. As disciples ourselves, though it may be unworthy of the name, and as distant from *them* in merit as we are in time, yet as professed disciples of that heavenly Master, we are naturally curious to learn more than simply the names of our favored predecessors. We would make ourselves acquainted with those men who saw, and heard, and touched, and lived and conversed with, that holy prophet of God, for whom we feel a reverence only inferior to that which we entertain toward Him who sent him.

And who were those, we would ask, in the second place, who were appointed by Jesus Christ to publish his religion, and enabled by the assistance of the Holy Spirit of God to publish it successfully? Who were those, who, in obedience to their Master, went out into all nations, teaching, converting, and baptizing, and planting the parent churches of our faith in learned Greece, and lordly Rome, and benighted Africa, and among those rude people of the North from whom we ourselves are descended? It was no mean work in which they were employed. No revolution of recorded time can equal it in glory; for thrones were subjected to its power, and the poor and humble of the earth were raised by it to an elevation far higher than thrones. They, like their Lord, were invested with a control over the operations of nature; and, more than that, they, like him, and by his authority, and with his instruction, founded an empire, the most broad and lasting which has ever existed, over the human mind. Who were they? As Christians, as subjects of that empire, as men amazed, at the same time that we are rejoiced, at what we have heard and what we behold, we are impelled to inquire who they were who established a dominion which has already covered the civilized world, and is apparently going on, with ever-encroaching steps, to spread itself over the whole earth. If the lives of any men are interesting, theirs must be peculiarly so. They are the great reformers, the great conquerors, whose empire has been continually increasing and strengthening, while the houses and dynasties of heroes and kings have risen, and flourished, and passed away into forgetfulness and ruin; the only empire which has grown more vigorous and more hopeful with age, because the mind and the heart and the destiny of man, and the good providence of God, are joined to support and perpetuate it. Who were these men?

No elaborate biography, no studied panegyric, has portrayed to us the lives and characters of the apostles of Christ. In their own condensed and simple writings, and in the quite as simple book of their Acts, composed by one of their associates, we must glean such sketches of them as are to be found in connection with the accounts of their Master and the history of their religion; for of themselves, as individuals, they seldom think of speaking; absorbed in their duty and devoted to their great work, the idea of self-importance or personal fame never seems to have entered their minds. We shall not, however, esteem them the less because they were faithful to their calling, and sought not the praise and honor of men, and postponed their own glory to the glory of God. And although our just curiosity may not be gratified by a full and detailed portraiture of these eminent men, who remembered their work, and forgot themselves, yet we shall meet with notices enough in the Scriptures of the New Testament to enable us to form for ourselves an outline at least of some of their lives and characters. Of some of them we shall find more abundant accounts than of others; for among them, as well as among mankind in general, there was undoubtedly a diversity of power, which caused some of them to stand out in the foreground of action, and others to remain comparatively in shade; though all of them might have been zealous, useful, and efficient, and most probably were so.

Though the sacred writings themselves are the only sources of knowledge on this subject to which we may give implicit credence, yet from other early documents we may obtain some narratives of the latter days of the apostles which are worthy of a good degree of faith. Making use, therefore, of such authorities as are within my reach, I shall proceed to give some account of the twelve disciples of our Lord; pursuing the order in which they are arranged by Matthew, only because his catalogue is the first which occurs in the common collocation of the Gospel histories.

SIMON PETER.

SIMON, who also received from our Lord the appellation of Peter, is invariably the first named on all the four lists of the apostles, and was, on several accounts, the chief of their company. He was one of the first who was called to be a disciple; though not the very first, for Andrew his brother appears to have been called before him, or at least at the same time with him. He was distinguished above the rest by the solemn predictions and trusts of his Master, by his uncommon zeal, and by his strong natural talents. He is altogether not only a conspicuous disciple, but a remarkable man. The sacred historians give us more copious accounts of him than of the other apostles, and a distinct conception of his character may be gained from what they relate.

He was, as is stated two or three times in the Gospels, the son of John or Jona, who was probably, like his children, a fisherman. The family had lived in the town of Bethsaida, on the northwestern side of the lake of Genesareth, otherwise called the sea of Tiberias, or the sea of Galilee,* where Peter was born; but they afterwards seem to have removed to the neighboring city of Capernaum, and then consisted, as far as we can ascertain, of Simon himself, his brother, and his father, his wife, and her mother. When Galilee was the scene of our Saviour's ministry, Capernaum was the place of his most constant abode; and it is probable that his resort to it was determined in some measure by its being the residence of Peter, in whose house he is thought to have lodged.

As we learn from the Evangelist John, Simon was acquainted with Jesus, and had heard him attentively, before he became one of the selected disciples. His brother Andrew was already one of the disciples of John the Baptist, and was standing with a fellow-disciple in company with their master, at a time when Jesus was passing by. Looking upon him as he walked, John, by whom he had recently been baptized, exclaimed, "Behold the Lamb of God!" Upon this, the two followed him, and, on the invitation of Jesus, went with him to his dwelling-place, and abode with him that day. Convinced of the justice of his claims, Andrew sought for his brother Simon, and

---

* This lake took its name of *Galilee* from the province in which it was situated, and *Genesareth* and *Tiberias* from towns on its coast. It was more anciently called the sea of Chinnereth. Numb. xxxiv. 11; Josh. xiii. 27.

saying to him, "We have found the Messias, or Christ," he brought him to Jesus. And when Jesus beheld them, he said, "Thou art Simon, the son of Jona; thou shalt be called Cephas," which is by interpretation into the Greek, Petra, and into English, a Rock. By this manner of receiving Simon, Jesus manifested that he was acquainted with him, and had formed an estimate of his character; that he had marked him as one who was fitted by his energy and activity to establish his religion on durable foundations; that even now he intended him for a great work. The brothers may at this early period be considered as disciples or pupils of Jesus, though not yet chosen, according to the language of St. Mark, to "be with him always"; for they still continued fishermen. It is pleasant to know that the two who were first called to be disciples were united together by the tie of natural brotherhood; that the one brother led the other to the Saviour; that they pursued their simple occupation together; and that together they were called from that simple occupation to become fishers of men.

That event took place a short time after, in the following manner. As Jesus stood by the lake, surrounded by a crowd who were pressing upon him to hear the word of God, he saw Simon and Andrew, in the practice of their usual occupation, and washing their nets on the shore. He entered their vessel, and prayed them to thrust out a little from the land, that he might the more conveniently teach the people. Then, having finished his discourse, he bade them launch out into the deep, and let down their net for a draught of fishes. It is now that we begin to perceive the ardent, affectionate, and confiding character of Peter. Though he and his companions had been toiling through the night without the least success, yet he at once consented to make another effort, in obedience to the wishes of Jesus. "Nevertheless, at thy word," he says, "I will let down the net." This was no sooner done than such a multitude of fishes were enclosed, that the net began to break, and they were obliged to call their partners, who were in another ship, to assist them, and both ships were so filled with what they drew in as to be near sinking. On beholding this, Simon Peter, ever a man of impulses, "fell down at Jesus' knees, saying, Depart from me, for I am a sinful man, O Lord." In a transport of fearful humility he beseeches Jesus to leave him, and not to stay with one so unworthy of his holy and wonderful presence. But Jesus, instead of leaving him, now gives him the call to his apostleship, saying to him, "Fear not; from henceforth thou shalt catch men"; or, as the other evangelists write, applying the words to both the brethren, "I will make you fishers of men." Readily accepting the invitation to become the constant companions of the Messiah, and perhaps secretly expecting worldly advantage from their connection with so great a personage, they straightway left all, their property, their home, and their former friends, and followed him.

Peter's character now rapidly unfolds itself; a character of strong and contrasted features; bold, honest, and vehement, and yet wavering and inconstant; now forward and daring before all his companions, and now more timid than any of them. Wherever we meet with him, it is the same Simon that we see; distinguished alike for high and generous virtues, and for faults inconsistent with those virtues, and altogether unworthy of them. Strength and weakness, courage and irresolution, impetuosity and indecision, are mixed up in his temperament in a striking and yet perfectly natural combination; and at the bottom of the whole there is a purity of feeling, and an integrity of purpose, which endear him to his Master, and fit him at last for his important destination and office.

One of the occasions which may be noticed as developing these characteristics is that of his attempt to walk on the sea to meet Jesus. We are informed that after the miracle of the loaves and fishes, which took place on one side of the lake, Jesus commanded his disciples to pass over to the other in a vessel, while he remained to send the multitude away. A storm overtook the ship when she was in the midst of the sea, and, while she was tossing on the waves, Jesus came to them in the fourth watch of the night, or towards morning, walking on the sea, as on dry land. At this extraordinary sight the disciples were troubled, saying, " It is a spirit "; and to such a height was their terror excited, that they cried out for fear. But Jesus immediately spoke to them, and bade them not to be afraid, for it was himself. No sooner does Peter hear his voice, than he not only dismisses his fear, but gives loose to his enthusiasm, and unwilling to wait till his Master reaches the vessel, and perhaps, too, tempted a little to display his faith, and do some great thing, he exclaims, before the others have recovered the use of their speech, " Lord, if it be thou, bid me come unto thee on the water." And Jesus, knowing him perfectly, and willing at once to gratify, to test, and to instruct him, said, " Come." Peter descends from the ship, and walks towards his Master. But the storm was stronger than his trust; and when he felt himself out, so strangely and awfully, amidst the dashing foam and the boisterous wind, he was afraid, and he forgot his confidence; and his faith, which hitherto had borne him up, grew faint and unable to hold him, and, beginning to sink, he cried again, and with the voice of despair, to Jesus, " Lord, save me ! " " And immediately Jesus stretched forth his hand and caught him, and said unto him, O thou of little faith, wherefore didst thou doubt ? " That was all the Saviour said; that mild rebuke, so unlike the denunciations which his professed followers in other ages have launched at what they have been pleased to call, but could not with certainty know to be, deficiencies of faith; that mild rebuke from him who did know all things was the only punishment for the failing faith of the disciple, — " Wherefore didst thou doubt ? " Wherefore, after seeing what thou hast seen, and hearing what thou hast heard, couldst thou doubt? And he raised the self-convicted man, and brought him into the ship, and " the wind ceased."

Notwithstanding Simon's occasional misgivings and temporary weaknesses, his fidelity was in the main firm and certain, because it was founded on the real goodness and tenderness of his nature. There was a time, when, as related in the sixth chapter of the Gospel of John, many of the followers of Jesus " went back, and walked no more with him," because he spoke to them obscurely and figuratively of his office and kingdom, and because, from what they did understand, they began to suspect that there was something much more spiritual and much less lucrative and splendid in his proposed dominion than suited with their earthly conceptions. They went back, therefore, and walked no more with him. Then said Jesus unto the twelve, his chosen twelve, "Will ye also go away?" To whose heart, of those twelve hearts, does the affecting appeal first find its way? Who answers it first? The same man who but just now was afraid of the wind. "Then Simon Peter answered him, Lord, to whom shall we go? thou hast the words of eternal life. And we believe and are sure that thou art that Christ, the Son of the living God." Generous, full-hearted, though too inconstant disciple! Though others desert that good and gentle Master, thou wilt not leave him. In this time of trial thy heart has kept thee right. Thou art like some tall and comely tree, whose pliant trunk is swayed hither and thither by the passing storm, but whose tenacious root spreads wide abroad, and pierces deep beneath, and still reclaims the waving plant, and binds it firmly to the soil it loves.

At yet another time also, Peter made the same open and bold confession. It was when Jesus, having asked his disciples whom men said that he was, and having received their answer, put the question to them, saying, "But whom say ye that I am?" Again it is the ardent Simon who advances before the rest, and answers unhesitatingly,

"Thou art the Christ, the Son of the living God." This renewed proof of his attachment and faith draws forth the marked approbation of his Master, who answered him and said, "Blessed art thou, Simon, son of Jona; for flesh and blood hath not revealed it unto thee, but my Father who is in heaven. The Spirit of God, himself, hath enlightened thee. And I say also unto thee, that thou art Peter. I have already called thee a rock, and upon this rock will I build my church, and the gates of the place of death shall not prevail against it. Upon thy exertions shall the foundations of my church be laid, and laid so strongly that they shall never be overturned nor destroyed. And I will give unto thee the keys of the kingdom of heaven; and whatsoever thou shalt bind on earth shall be bound in heaven; and whatsoever thou shalt loose on earth shall be loosed in heaven."

That by these words of Jesus a certain degree of apostolic pre-eminence was conferred on Peter, I think is too plain to be disputed; though some over-zealous Protestants have denied the fact. But why they should wish to deny it, I cannot see; for I cannot see how the primacy which his Lord chose to confer on him should disturb them; nor can I see, on the other hand, how that primacy, being fully admitted, can be an argument for the papal supremacy. If Peter was thought by his Master worthy of standing first among his disciples, who shall say that he did not deserve the dignity? But what was the nature of that dignity? "On this rock will I build my church," said Jesus. The Christian Church was not built on Peter alone, nor by him alone; for all the apostles contributed to the edifice; but to Peter was commissioned the duty of first declaring the Gospel to the Jews, and indeed, by a special vision, to the Gentiles also; and the centurion and his family, converted and baptized by him, were the first fruits of Christianity out of the Jewish pale. He was, therefore, the foundation of the Church, — the rock on which its beginnings were laid. But there is nothing transferable in this part of his dignity, at least. The foundations of the Church are not to be laid twice and thrice, and over and over again, because a series of men calling themselves popes claim to be his successors. Neither is there any promise of transmitting the keys of the kingdom of heaven, which signify only that authority which Peter, as an accredited apostle of Christ, was to have in his ministry. He was empowered to act in general as an ambassador from Heaven; to enact regulations, to establish and to break down, to do and to undo, with the concurrence and power of the Head of the Church himself. And this authority, let it be remembered, was committed to all the rest of the apostles in precisely the same words; for they also were to preach their Master's doctrine to the world, and needed his delegated power in things pertaining to his kingdom. To them also did he say, therefore, "Whatsoever ye shall bind on earth shall be bound in heaven; and whatsoever ye shall loose on earth shall be loosed in heaven." The pre-eminence of Peter, then, appears to be simply a precedence among his brethren and equals, which was conceded to his abilities and energy; and a preference which was bestowed on him as a teacher of the religion of Christ. But there is no promise, no intimation, in the Scriptures, that even this pre-eminence was to descend on other men; nor does the similarity between the popes of Rome and Simon Peter of Bethsaida — between the triple-crowned sovereigns of Christendom, who once set their feet on kings' necks, and the plain fisherman of the sea of Galilee — seem to be, in any point of view, very close or striking.

Whatever elation of heart may have been produced in Peter by the praise of a beloved Master, it was almost immediately doomed to be checked and mortified by the same impartial voice; for in the very chapter which records this last occurrence, we are told that the disciple drew upon himself one of the severest rebukes which Jesus ever uttered. "From that time forth," says the Evangelist, "began Jesus to show unto his disciples, how that he must go unto Jerusalem, and suffer many things of the elders and chief priests and scribes, and be killed, and be raised again the third day." Intimations of this kind were always peculiarly unwelcome and enigmatical to the disciples; and on this occasion Peter came forward as usual, and with even more than his usual warmth took up his Master, and began to rebuke him, saying, " Be it far from thee, Lord; this shall not be unto thee." Though he had so lately acknowledged Jesus to be the Messiah, and had adhered to him in his humble and unkingly condition, yet even he had not wholly disjoined the ideas of worldly power and dignity from the person and office of the expected Saviour; and the thought of his violent and shameful death was altogether shocking to him. But Jesus was particularly anxious to crush these misapprehensions, and to familiarize his followers to his real situation and his approaching and inevitable fate. He therefore thought proper before them all to express, in a manner which might make them feel, how earnest his disapprobation was of their temporal expectations and fancies. "He turned, and said unto Peter, Get thee behind me, Satan [tempter, adversary]; thou art an offence unto me; for thou savorest not the things that be of God, but those that be of men." The disciples had yet to learn, Simon Peter had yet to learn, how pure, unearthly, and immortal that religion was which they were appointed one day to promulgate; how it associated itself more with human suffering than with human glory and pride; more with the secret sympathies and internal affections, much more than with the outward adornments of our nature; and the early death of their Master — an event which they could not bear to think, and could hardly conceive of, but which he, the Divine Master, saw with a clear and steady vision — was yet to teach them that the infant doctrine which was to go through the world, consoling the sorrows of the mourner, and pouring balm into wounded bosoms, was itself first to be nurtured with tears and baptized in blood.

There is no doubt that Peter received his Master's rebuke properly, for we find that he was still distinguished and confided in by him. He, together with James and John, was selected to witness the transfiguration on the mount; and in the same company he had also witnessed the resurrection of the daughter of Jairus. It appears, moreover, that about this time he and his Lord dwelt together at Capernaum, in the same house; for when the gatherers of the annual tribute came to Peter, he went into the house, and was there told by Jesus how he was to obtain a piece of money which would pay for them both. It would appear, therefore, that they lived together, and, if so, that the disciple was high in the favor and confidence of his Master. He seems also to have exercised a sort of conceded pre-eminence among the twelve, as we often find him speaking in their name and behalf, both in asking and in answering questions. His rank is now evidently fixed. He is honored by his Master, notwithstanding his imperfections, and he is the head of the apostles, both from appointment and character.

But his fault of impetuosity is not yet mended. It is one of the last faults, perhaps, which ever is mended, because it is constitutional. On that most solemn night of the last supper, Jesus, in order that he might at once testify his affection for his disciples, whom he loved unto the end, and show them also an example of practical humility, began to wash their feet, as if he had been their servant. When he came to Peter, that disciple, hurt and grieved that his Master should undertake so menial an office, gives way to his feelings, again presumes to dictate to that very Master, and exclaims, "Lord, dost thou wash my feet?" Jesus condescends to expostulate with him, and to assure him that he would soon explain to him the act which now appeared so strange. "What I do, thou knowest not now, but thou shalt know hereafter." But Peter will not yield, nor listen, but answers, "Thou shalt never wash my feet." To which Jesus replies, "If I wash thee not, thou hast no part with me." That is, "If you will not receive this symbolical lesson of humility; if you cannot cease your disputes about who shall be greatest in my kingdom; if you will not divest yourselves of your notions of place and dignity, and become lowly, meek, and mutually kind, as my disciples ought to be, and must be, if they desire my approbation, then I must discard you from my service, and deprive you of my friendship." Peter, subdued at the bare intimation of forfeiting his Master's esteem, and again driven beyond the just limits of duty by the sudden revulsion of his ungoverned feelings, cries out, "Lord, not my feet only, but my hands and my head. Wash me all over, if it be thy will, only take not from me thy love." How perfectly natural is the whole of this scene; how consistent with the previous character of Peter; how just to the character of his Lord!

And now the time draws near when the first of the apostles is to be tried more severely and to fall more sadly than ever. Soon after Jesus had washed his disciples' feet, he began to talk to them, in a most affecting strain, of his speedy death and his return to his Father. Peter's feelings are again alarmed, and he declares that, wherever his Master may go, he will follow him, and go with him, even into prison and to death. "Though all men shall be offended because of thee, yet I will never be offended; I will lay down my life for thy sake." Jesus, better aware of his disciple's weakness, and knowing that it would not be equal to the approaching trial, mournfully answered, "Wilt thou lay down thy life for my sake? Verily, verily, I say unto thee, the cock shall not crow till thou hast denied me thrice." And yet the ardent disciple spoke the more vehemently, and said, "Though I should die with thee, yet will I not deny thee."

Let us mark the result. After discoursing to his disciples, in those beautiful words which are to be found in the fourteenth, fifteenth, and sixteenth chapters of the Gospel of John, Jesus went out with them, and, coming to a place which was named Gethsemane, left them there, and, taking with him Peter, James, and John, to watch with him, withdrew apart to pray to his Father. When he returned to these favored three, he found them, not watching, but asleep. It was towards morning; and with frames oppressed with fatigue, and minds made heavy with sorrow, they had not been able to watch with their suffering and agonized Lord during his short absence, but had sunk down in a leaden slumber. More in pity than in wrath, the Saviour, addressing himself particularly to Peter, as the individual who had boasted the loudest, and had the most need of warning, said to him, "What! could ye not watch with me one hour? After all your professions, can you not banish sleep, and prove your attachment, by a vigil, for my sake, of one short hour? Watch and pray, that ye enter not into temptation; the spirit indeed is full of courage, but the flesh is weak." Again and again he returns to them, and still finds them sleeping. Then comes the traitor Judas, with his band, and they are roused effectually; and Peter, who could not watch for his Master at his earnest request, undertakes, without his authority, to fight for him; and he drew his sword, and smote a servant of the high priest, and cut off his ear. So much easier is it to fight than to be dutiful; and so much the more readily could Peter obey the impulses of his passions than the behest of his Lord. Jesus calmly reproves the offender, and then all his disciples forsook him and fled.

There were two, however, who did not wholly forsake him; but still, though at a distance, followed him. One of these two was Peter; he sincerely loved his Master, and, though just rebuked by him, he resolves not to lose sight of him, but follows him afar off, even into the court of the high priest's house. There, trembling, anxious, and vibrating between fear and affection, he takes his seat with the servants at the fire. He does not remain there long unsuspected, but is charged with being one of the followers of Jesus. His fear preponderates; his bold resolution, so lately formed, gave way; he denies all knowledge of his Master. Yes, Simon Peter, the leader of the twelve, the rock of the Church, the confidant of Jesus, who walked on the sea, who held the spiritual keys, who saw the dead raised up, who witnessed the glorious transfiguration, who declared himself but just now ready to be bound, and led to death for his Master, now sits among menials, denying him to menials! with the mingled flush of dread and shame upon his cheek, denying, to a set of scoffing hirelings of a corrupt palace, that he ever knew that kind and trusting Master whom he had so lately acknowledged to be the princely Messiah, the Son of the King of Heaven! By and by, and from another quarter, he is again attacked with the same charge, — "Thou also wast with Jesus of Nazareth." Having committed himself once, and not having recovered from his confusion and fear, detected, and yet obstinate, struggling between contrition and wrath, a deep sense of humiliation and a strong dread of exposure, he again "denied before them all, saying, I know not what thou sayest."

There are some apparent discrepancies in the several accounts given by the evangelists of Peter's denial of his Master. But they are only apparent; and indeed the veracity of the sacred writers is rather confirmed by these slight differences, which ought to be expected in separate narratives of what must necessarily have been a confused and hurried scene. John, for instance, says that Peter *stood* with the officers at the fire, and Matthew and Mark say that he *sat*. Doubtless he sat at one time and stood at another, in the agitation he was in, and therefore both relations are not only true, but more strikingly authentic from their very appearance of discrepancy. Again, there is a difference with regard to the persons who are represented as having at several times accused Peter. Now, it is highly probable that though the apostle made but three distinct denials, he was yet accused by many, who in a tumultuous manner may have raised their voices against him, and thus rendered it doubtful who was the prominent assailant among a number of clamorous witnesses. In short, the accounts of the evangelists are evidently but sketches of a scene in which many things occurred which are not related by either, and some things which are recorded by one, though omitted by another. The main facts, however, agree in all; and this being the case, the variations accord so well with the character of the scene described, and the agitation which all parties must have been in, that they only add truth to truth.

Only imagine the scene! Jesus, standing bound, as if he had been a criminal, surrounded by soldiers and exulting enemies, and questioned like an apprehended culprit by the high priest, but dignified, collected, and prepared for the worst; while just below is his chief disciple, in the midst of a servile crowd, agonized with terror, and endeavoring with all his native vehemence, and with a native accent too, which of itself contradicts him, to clear himself before his contemptible accusers from the imputation of having anything to do with one whom he had been following daily and hourly for months, and whom, but a few moments ago, he had promised to follow to prison and to death! But the measure of his degradation is not yet full; for again, the third time, is the charge repeated; "Surely, thou also art one of them, for thy speech betrayeth thee." And then, as others are apt to do, who become more boisterous the more they are in the wrong and the nearer they are to detection, and who call the God of truth to witness their transgressions of truth, the unhappy man "began to curse and to swear, saying, I know not the man. And immediately the cock crew." How dark is the account now of disgrace and crime against the fallen disciple! Ingratitude, cowardice, falsehood, profanity! It was the lowest fall; and, happily, it was the last. "The Lord turned, and looked upon Peter."

What a volume of pathos and eloquence is contained in those few simple words! His Lord looked upon him, "and with that gracious and chiding look called him back to himself and him." He remembered all,— remembered his Master's love, remembered his Master's warning, remembered his own duty. Conviction falls upon him, repentance overwhelms him, and he went out and wept bitterly.

> "What language in that look! Swifter than thought
> The apostle's eye it caught,
> And sank into his very soul!
> Through every vein a thrilling tremor crept;
> Away he stole,
> And wept;
> Bitterly he wept!"

From this time till after the crucifixion of Jesus, we hear no more of Peter. He probably passed this distressing interval in remorse and tears; and there is no doubt that his repentance was entire and sincere, and that his character was much improved and purified by the late fiery trial through which it had been led; for we find that Jesus, on the morning of his resurrection, after he had shown himself to Mary Magdalene, appeared also to Peter, according to an especial message which he had sent to him by an angel, in testimony of his continued confidence in him.* That Peter

---

* The message was delivered by the angel to the Marys, who reported it to Peter. The angel, or young man clothed in white,

had returned to his allegiance is manifest from the fact that he was the first of the male disciples who descended into the tomb wherein the Saviour had been laid.

Some days afterwards, as several of the disciples were fishing together in a vessel, on the sea of Tiberias, Jesus appeared to them on the shore. On this occasion we may again observe a symptom of Peter's characteristic ardor. No sooner had he understood from John that it was the Lord who stood on the shore, and had been speaking with them, than he girt his fisher's coat about him, cast himself into the sea, and in this manner gained the land, while the rest came after him in the vessel. When they had all dined on the fish which had been taken, Jesus required of Peter that thrice-repeated assurance of his love in which a fanciful interpreter would discover a direct allusion to the late thrice-repeated denial. On receiving each assurance, his Lord gives him an especial charge to feed his sheep. He then signified to

says to the women, "Tell his disciples, *and Peter*, that he goeth before you into Galilee; there shall ye see him, as he said unto you." What a touching pledge of forgiveness and reconciliation! The moral to be derived from the history of Peter's fall is thus well and concisely brought home to us in the following verse by Cowper: —

" Beware of Peter's word,
   Nor confidently say
'I never will deny thee, Lord,'
   But, 'Grant I never may!'"

him, though darkly, by what death he should glorify God; but refused to gratify his curiosity respecting the fate of his fellow-disciple John.

In the Gospels we have no further information respecting this apostle. On turning to the Book of Acts, however, he is immediately presented to us in his former rank and station, as chief of the apostles, speaking in their name, and presiding at their meetings. It is he who proposes that the vacated place of Judas Iscariot should be supplied by lot. When some of those who were present at the effusion of the Holy Spirit, and the gift of tongues, mocked at the disciples, and said that they were full of new wine, it was Peter who in a most spirited manner refuted the slander, and spoke so powerfully of his Master's claims, that on the same day there were added to the number of Christian believers about three thousand souls. It was Peter who healed the lame man at the Beautiful Gate of the temple; who addressed the people on that occasion; who, when arraigned before the chief priests, declared so boldly to them that salvation was alone by Jesus Christ; and who, when he and his companion John were commanded not to speak at all nor teach in that name, returned, jointly with the beloved disciple, that heroic answer, "Whether it be right in the sight of God to hearken unto you more than unto God, judge ye." It was Peter who exposed the deception of Ananias and his wife Sapphira, and at whose feet they both fell down dead. And it was Peter, who, by his shadow alone, healed many who were laid in his way.*

After Samaria had, through the instrumentality of Philip, received the word of God, Peter and John were sent there by the apostles, in order that they might lay their hands on the converts, and cause them to receive the Holy Spirit.† And then it was that Peter so indignantly rebuked Simon the sorcerer, who thought that the gift of

---

* It is not expressly asserted in Acts v. 15, that those persons were healed by Peter's shadow, and therefore some commentators have taken it for granted that they were not, and have even gone so far as to assert, that the apostle's neglect of them was a punishment for their superstition. So says Rosenmüller. But in the next verse we are told that great numbers of sick persons were also brought to him from the cities round about, and "were healed every one." Now there seems to be no good reason why these should be healed, and those who belonged to the city should be neglected. Their being placed in Peter's way, so that even his shadow might pass over them, shows more the affectionate and confident faith of them and their friends than it does their superstition. If Peter was empowered from on high to heal diseases, he could do so by his shadow, as well as by a touch or a few words. His will was the agent; the signs of its exertion were of no importance in themselves. As we are not informed that Peter rebuked those who laid the sick under his shadow, the most reasonable and compassionate inference is, that these, as well as the others, were healed.

† The fact that the apostles *sent* Peter on this mission is proof sufficient that his precedence among them was far from being of the *papal* character.

God might be purchased with money. "Thy money perish with thee," said he; "thou hast neither part nor lot in this matter, for thy heart is not right in the sight of God."

We now find him very actively engaged in the duties of his apostleship, "passing throughout all quarters," performing miracles, preaching the word, and feeding the sheep of the great Shepherd. At Lydda he healed a certain man, named Æneas, who had been sick with the palsy eight years; and at the neighboring town of Joppa he raised to life a pious female disciple by the name of Tabitha, or Dorcas.*

At Joppa he abode many days with one Simon, a tanner. It was while he was living here that he was called to instruct and baptize Cornelius, the centurion, who dwelt in Cæsarea; to prepare him for which duty, he was taught in a remarkable vision, not to call any creature of God common or unclean, and that God is no respecter of persons, but in every nation he that feareth him and worketh righteousness is accepted with him. With these convictions on his mind, he obeys the call of Cornelius to come to him, and, while he is addressing him, witnesses the descent of the Spirit on him and his family, and orders them to be baptized in the name of the Lord. Thus he fulfilled

* Tabitha being the Syriac name, and Dorcas its translation into Greek. The words mean a *doe* or *kid*.

to the utmost the prediction with which his name of Peter was conferred on him, and founded the Christian Church in both the Jewish and the Gentile world. It was an event of which we at this period can hardly estimate the importance. Devoid of Jewish prejudices and antipathies, we can hardly conceive with what consternation the Jewish converts, who, as Jews, had always cherished the belief that religion and truth and God's peculiar favor always had been, and always were to be, confined to them, must have listened to the intelligence that the chief of the apostles had been breaking down the wall and drawing up the veil which were interposed between the faithful people and the rest of the world, and that henceforth there was to be no spiritual distinction between Hebrew and Greek, Jew and Gentile. Some conception of this indignant surprise of theirs may be formed from the recorded circumstance, that when Peter had returned to Jerusalem, "they that were of the circumcision," including his fellow-apostles, and indeed the whole Christian Church, "contended with him, saying, thou wentest in to men uncircumcised, and didst eat with them." It was enough to provoke their amazement, that he simply eat with them. But Peter had the steadfastness to defend himself, and expound the whole matter to them from the beginning; and so much were they impressed by the force and reason of his words, that they acquiesced in peace, " and glorified God, saying, Then hath God also to the Gentiles granted repentance unto life."

Not long after this, Peter was put into prison by Herod, but was set free by an angel, who came to him while he " was sleeping between two soldiers, bound with two chains." That he was sleeping in such a situation is an incidental and beautiful proof of his tranquillity in extreme danger. He then went down from Judæa to Cæsarea, and there abode; very probably in the house or under the protection of Cornelius, his distinguished convert.

The next time that we hear of him is at the meeting of apostles and elders, which is generally called the Council of Jerusalem, and which was convened to settle the long and vehemently agitated question, again brought up by some of the believing Pharisees, whether it was needful to circumcise all converts, and command them to keep the law of Moses. When there had been much disputing, Peter rose up, and gave his decided opinion against the necessity of circumcising the Gentiles, or bringing them under the ceremonial law. And with this opinion the Council at last coincided.

With the history of this Council, the notices of Peter's life in the Acts of the Apostles come to an

E

end. He is named a few times in the epistles of Paul, and once with reprehension. That apostle tells us in his Epistle to the Galatians, that, when Peter was come to Antioch,* he withstood him to the face because he was to be blamed; for that although he had already eaten with Gentiles, according to his own new principles so openly professed, yet when some of the circumcision came to Antioch, he withdrew from the Gentiles, from fear of the circumcised. This was an inconsistency, certainly, and shows that some remains of weakness still lingered about the character of Peter; but it is the only inconsistency which is laid to his charge from the time of his Master's resurrection; and he can easily be forgiven, when we consider how much he had done and suffered, ever since that event, in his Master's name and for his Master's cause.

All that remains to be said of this remarkable man is to be gathered, not from the Scriptures, but from other early accounts, the authority of

* Ecclesiastical historians say that Peter founded the Church at Antioch, and some add, that he was its first bishop. Chrysostom writes: "This is one prerogative of our city (Antioch), that we had at the beginning the chief of the apostles for our master. For it was fit that the place which was first honored with the name of Christians should have the chief of the apostles for its pastor. But though we had him for a master awhile, we did not detain him, but resigned him to the royal city, Rome. Or, rather, we have him still. For though we have not his body, we have his faith." — *Chrysostom*, as adduced by Lardner.

which, though not to be compared with that of the Scriptures, should be held in a due degree of respect. We are informed by Eusebius, that Origen wrote of him, that "he was supposed to have preached to the Jews of the dispersion in Pontus, Galatia, Bithynia, Cappadocia, and Asia. And at length coming to Rome, was crucified with his head downwards." This kind of death he was said to have requested, out of a feeling of humble respect to his Master. If so, it is an affecting conclusion of his eventful life, and another striking exhibition of the ardent character which adhered to him to the last. He conceived it too great an honor that such an one as he should meet his death erect, and looking upwards, like his beloved and venerated Lord; and so, with his head in the dust, he closed his labors, his failings, his victories, his sufferings, and his life.

There are Roman Catholic writers who maintain that Peter was bishop of Rome during a period of twenty-five years before his martyrdom there. But this assertion, though supported by such high authority as that of Jerome, has been shown by Cave and others to be wholly unfounded. The most authentic account is, that Peter, after having been in Antioch for a season, came to Rome about the year 63 or 64, and suffered martyrdom in the manner above stated, a year or two after, during the persecution of the Christians by the tyrant Nero, and that St. Paul was martyred there at the same time. It also seems probable that he was crucified and buried on the Vatican Hill, whence his remains were afterwards removed to the Catacombs in the neighborhood of the city. Caias, a writer quoted by Eusebius, states that in his time, about the year 200, the tombs of Peter and Paul were to be seen at Rome, which is very likely to be true. It is the belief of the Catholics, that the body of Peter now reposes under the splendid church which is called by his name: —

"Christ's mighty shrine above his martyr's tomb!"

Cave inclines to the opinion that neither Peter nor Paul was, properly speaking, bishop of the Roman Church. He supposes that by their united exertions they planted it, and that its first bishop was Linus, who by the Catholics is placed next to St. Peter in the episcopal see. Irenæus, about 178, speaks of the Church of Rome as "founded and established by the two great apostles, Peter and Paul." But Epiphanius calls them the first apostles *and bishops* of Rome; after whom, he says, were Linus, Cletus, Clement.

The following description of the person of St. Peter, by Nicephorus, an ecclesiastical historian of the early part of the fourteenth century, is entitled to very little credence. But it may be regarded as a curiosity, if not a true portrait. "His body was somewhat slender, of a middle size, but rather inclining to tallness; his complexion very pale and almost white; the hair of his head and beard curled and thick, but withal short; though St. Jerome tells us that he was bald, which probably might be in his declining age; his eyes black, but specked with red; his eyebrows thin, or none at all; his nose long, but rather broad and flat than sharp."

It is certain that he was a married man, and probable that his wife accompanied him in his journeys. St. Paul is thought to intimate as much, when he says, in his First Epistle to the Corinthians (ix. 5.): "Have we not power to lead about a sister, a wife, as well as other apostles, and as the brethren of the Lord, and Cephas?"

That he was married when he was called to be an apostle is certain, as the Scriptures mention his "wife's mother." But stanch Catholics, with Jerome at their head, will have it that he left his wife when he left all to follow Jesus. This, however, does not well agree with the testimony of Paul. Clemens Alexandrinus relates, that Peter, seeing his wife going to be martyred, exceedingly rejoiced that she was elected to so great an honor, and that she was now returning home; and, calling her by her name, encouraged and exhorted her, bidding her to be mindful of our Lord. The apostle is also said to have had a daughter by the name of Petronilla.

Two epistles of Peter are received into the Canon of the New Testament. The authenticity of the first is well established and generally allowed. It is addressed "to the strangers scattered throughout Pontus, Galatia, Cappadocia, Asia, and Bithynia." By these "strangers" is most probably meant the Jewish Christians who sojourned in those regions; though some commentators would have the term to apply both to Jewish and Gentile converts. The epistle was written from Rome, which is figuratively denominated Babylon, in the concluding salutation. Its purpose was to strengthen and comfort those to whom it was addressed, who were suffering under the persecutions which had begun to be fiercely waged against them by the heathens. The topics urged in it are equal to its design, and are highly consolatory and animating. Of the whole epistle, Erasmus says: "It is worthy of the Prince of the apostles, and full of apostolical dignity and authority. It is sparing in words, but full of sense."

The genuineness of the second epistle has been called in question from early times. It never was fully disproved, however; and there was good reason for numbering it at last among the sacred books. The testimony of Eusebius concerning it is as follows: "One epistle of Peter, called his first, is acknowledged. This the presbyters of ancient times have quoted in their writings as undoubtedly genuine. But that called his second, we have been informed by tradition, has not been received as a part of the New Testament. Nevertheless, appearing to many to be useful, it hath been carefully studied with the other Scriptures." Origen, who flourished in the third century, says of the two epistles: "Peter, on whom the Church is built, hath left an epistle universally acknowledged. Let it be granted that he has also written a second; for it is doubted." That it was doubted is no proof of anything more than that the evidence in its favor was not so complete as that which could be produced for other sacred books. And it may be said, both of this epistle and the few other writings of the canon which were not fully received, that they manifest in their history how careful the first Christians were in examining the claims of alleged apostolical compositions, and adopting them as of authority in the Church. The learned and candid Lardner observes, that so well founded was the judgment of those early Christians concerning the books of the New Testament, that no writing which was by them pronounced genuine has, since their time, been found spurious; neither have we, at this day, the least reason to think any book genuine which they rejected.

We may be authorized, therefore, in accepting the second epistle of Peter as his true work, notwithstanding the rather doubtful character of its evidence. If it was written by him, it was probably written to the same persons, and from the same place, with the first. It was written, also, not long after the first, and not long before the death of the apostle.

The day consecrated to St. Peter as that of his martyrdom, in the Roman Calendar, to which the Calendar of the English Church corresponds, is June 29.

ANDREW.

OF Andrew, the brother of Simon Peter, we are told but little in the sacred writings; not enough, indeed, to enable us to form any estimate of his character. We may be permitted to conjecture, however, from the circumstance of his having been a disciple of John the Baptist, and also from his having gone voluntarily to hear the instructions of Jesus, and thus made himself his first disciple among those who were afterwards his apostles, — we may conjecture, I say, from these circumstances, which have already been stated in the life of Peter, that the temperament of Andrew was sober and religious, and that his mind was remarkably open to the reception of truth. So far as we can argue at all, we may argue the existence of everything that is good, from such commendable appearances. We can easily believe that he was a serious, candid, steadfast man; very probably without the shining talents and the burning zeal of his brother, and quite as probably without his brother's prominent faults. That not much is recorded of him is a proof that he was not very forward or active among the twelve; but it is by no means a proof that he wanted good sense, discretion, or stability.

We may also confidently deduce the affectionateness of this apostle's character from the circumstance of his seeking his brother, first of all, with that eager exclamation, "We have found the Messiah!" This fact alone would be enough to interest us in him, did we know nothing of him beside. After spending part of a day with Jesus in his place of abode, and being satisfied that he was the long-looked-for Redeemer, he does not shut up this knowledge in his own breast, and feed upon the honor alone; neither does he go and make himself of consequence by blazoning the matter abroad; but he hastens to share the pleasure and the confidence with his brother. "He *first* findeth his *own brother* Simon, and saith unto him, We have found the Messiah. And he brought him to Jesus." His joy was increased by his thus imparting it; and so will our piety be strengthened by communication. Who, that has truly found Jesus, will not desire, after the example of Andrew, to lead a brother to his blessed abode? And who that succeeds in leading a brother there will not feel that he crosses the sacred threshold with more delight and confidence than before?

Andrew is generally styled by the ancient writers of the Church *Protocletos*, or *the first called*. The following encomium on him is by Hesychius, Presbyter of Jerusalem: " St Andrew was the first-born of the Apostolic Choir ; the prime pillar of the Church ; a rock before the rock ; the foundation of that foundation ; the first fruits of the beginning ; a caller of others before he was called himself. He preached that Gospel which was not yet believed or entertained ; revealed and made known that life to his brother which he had not yet perfectly learned himself. So great treasures did that one question bring him, '·Master, where dwellest thou ?' which he soon perceived by the answer given him, and which he deeply pondered in his mind, ' Come and see.'"

We find, further, concerning him, that he was the disciple who, just before the miracle of feeding the five thousand, informed Jesus that there was a lad present who had five barley loaves and two small fishes, and then added the question, " But what are they among so many ? " This question, on the first view of it, seems to denote that Andrew had no idea that it was practicable to feed the multitude, and merely mentioned the small quantity of provisions in despair, and as an aggravation of their condition ; but it is possible, too, that he may have entertained a secret hope that it was in his Master's power to relieve their wants even with the five loaves and two fishes, and that he propounded the question in a hesitating manner, that he might draw forth his Master's intentions. If this last is the fact, it shows that he possessed more faith than was often manifested by the other disciples, though not such an enthusiastic faith as was sometimes displayed by his more ardent brother.

We read also of Andrew, that when certain Greeks, who had come up to Jerusalem to worship at the feast of the Passover, expressed to Philip their desire to see Jesus, Philip mentioned the request to Andrew, and then they went both together to impart it to Jesus. These Greeks were no doubt what were called Proselytes of the Gate, or Greeks who had been converted to the acknowledgment and worship of the true God; but who, on account of their Gentile extraction, were not entitled to all the religious privileges and distinctions of native Jews. They had heard of the fame of Jesus, and desired to be introduced to his presence, not only to gratify their curiosity, but, if we may judge from the succeeding discourse of our Saviour, to inquire concerning his kingdom. The precaution which was used by Philip in preferring their request is a sign, in the first place, that he was doubtful whether a Gentile ought to be brought into the company of the Messiah; and, secondly, that Andrew was, in his opinion, a person with whom he might profitably consult, in an affair which appeared to him to be of some moment and delicacy.

It was a few days after this that Andrew, together with Peter, James, and John, asked Jesus, privately, what the sign should be, when all the things which he had just been telling them respecting the destruction of the temple should be fulfilled. This is all which is related of this apostle in the Gospels. In no other part of the writings of the New Testament is he ever mentioned, excepting as he is included in the mention of the apostles as a body.

Other ancient accounts inform us that he preached the Gospel in Scythia, Byzantium or Constantinople, various provinces of Greece, and other countries and cities. At Sinope, on the Euxine Sea, he is said to have met with his brother Peter. At last, coming to Patræ in Achaia, now Patras, an archiepiscopal see, he was crucified there, by order of Agæus, proconsul of that province. On approaching the cross to which he was condemned to be bound with cords, that his death might be more lingering, he is said, by one of the ancients, to have apostrophized it in the following ardent manner: " Hail, precious cross, which has been consecrated by the body of my Lord! how ardently have I loved thee! how long have I sought thee!

at length I have found thee, now waiting to receive my longing soul. Take and snatch me from among mortals, and present me to my Master, that he who redeemed me on thee may receive me at thy hands."

The instrument of his martyrdom is commonly affirmed to have been what is called a *cross decussate*, made by two pieces of timber crossing each other in the middle, in the form of the letter X, and hence known by the name of St. Andrew's Cross.

His body was afterwards removed to Constantinople, and he is considered by the modern Greeks as founder of the Byzantine or Constantinopolitan Church.

Andrew is also the patron saint of Scotland; and the Scotch had a tradition that his remains were brought to their country, and entombed at St. Andrew's, in the fourth century. The day reserved to him in the Calendar is November 30. This day leads the season of Advent; and the honor of thus announcing the time of the Lord's coming is said to be assigned to him, on account of his having been the first who came to Christ.

JAMES THE GREATER.

James, the son of Zebedee, and the brother of John, is the third named on Matthew's list of the apostles. Of his father we are told nothing; but his mother, as appears by a comparison of parallel passages, was Salome, who emulated her children in attachment to the Saviour, and is spoken of as one of those women who followed and occasionally served him, who accompanied him to the cross, and were the first who were permitted to see him after his resurrection. This James has received the surname of the Greater, or Elder, to distinguish him from the other apostle, James the Less, of whom I shall speak hereafter.

He, with his brother John, pursued the same occupation with their townsmen Peter and Andrew, and were partners with them. They were also washing their nets on the shore, when Jesus entered the vessel of their partners. They beheld the miraculous draught of fishes; they assisted to secure it; they were astonished at it, and when Jesus, after calling Peter and Andrew, called them also, " they immediately left the ship and their father, and followed him."

Here I cannot help requesting my readers to pause a moment, and consider the fortunes, the singular, and, if the word were holy enough, I would say romantic, fortunes of these four men. Simon and Andrew, James and John, brethren of two different families, dwell together with their parents in a village at the northern extremity of a lake or small sea, in the district of Galilee, and on the confines of the land of Judæa. The sea is a large sea to them, and to them the towns which here and there dot its coast, and the light barks which, for the purposes of amusement, or traffic, or their own calling, skim along its pleasant waters, are the world. They are fishermen. Day by day do they rise up to the contented exercise of their toil, to throw their nets, to spread their sails, to ply their oars, and, when successful in pursuit, to dispose of their freight in their native village or the neighboring towns, for the support of themselves and their families. They are friends, partners; they have joined themselves to each other in their humble profession, and agreed to share profit and loss, storm and calm, together. Their low-roofed dwellings look out on each other and on their native lake, and within these dwellings are bosoms which throb anxiously at their protracted absence, and beat gladly at their return. Their boats contain all their wealth, and their cottages all that they love. Their fathers, perhaps their ancestors, were fishers before them. They themselves have no idea of a different lot. The only changes on which they calculate are the changes of the weather and the vicissitudes of their calling; and the only great interruptions of the even courses of their lives, to which they look forward, are the annual journeys which they take, at the periods of solemn festival, to the great city of Jerusalem. Thus they live, and thus they expect to live, till they lie down to sleep with their fathers, as calmly, as unknowing, and as unknown as they.

Look at them, on the shore of their lake. Think not of them as apostles, as holy men; but look at them as they actually were on the morning when you first hear of them from the historian. They have been toiling through a weary night, and have caught nothing; and now, somewhat disheartened at their ill success, they are engaged in spreading their nets, washing them, and preparing them, as they hope, for a more fortunate expedition. Presently surrounded by an eager crowd, that teacher approaches whom they have before seen, and whose instructions some of them have already listened to. With his demeanor of quiet but irresistible dignity, he draws toward the spot where they are employed; he enters Simon's vessel, and prays him to thrust out a little distance from the land; then he speaks to that assembled multitude as never man spake; then he bids Simon launch out farther, and cast his net in the deep; then follows the overwhelming draught of fishes; and then those four partners, filled with wonder and awe, are called to quit their boats, and throw by their nets, and become fishers of men.

And now what a change, like the change of a dream or of enchantment, has passed over their lives, dividing what was from what was to be! It was long before they themselves were aware how entire and how stupendous it was. In a few years they are to be the principal actors in the most extraordinary events of recorded time. Home, kindred, country, are to be forsaken forever. Their nets may hang and bleach in the sun; their boats may rot piecemeal on the shore; for the owners of them are far away, sailing over seas to which that of Genesareth is a pond; exciting whole cities and countries to wonder and tumult; answering before kings; imprisoned, persecuted, tortured; their whole existence a storm, and a greater one than ever swept over their lake. On the peaceful shore of that lake even their bones may not rest. Their ashes are to be separated from the ashes of their kindred. Their blood is to be sprinkled on foreign soils; the headsman and executioner are to preside over their untimely obsequies. A few years more, and the fame and the doctrine of these fishermen have gone out into all lands. Magnificent churches are called by their names. Kingdoms adopt them for their tutelar saints; and the men who claim to succeed to the office of one of them rule for centuries over all civilized kingdoms with a despotic and overshadowing sway, and by virtue of that claim give away a continent, a world, which, when their predecessor lived, was entirely unknown. History tells us of a fisherman of Sicily who was raised to that island's throne; but who will compare that or any earthly throne to the twelve thrones which were set up over the twelve tribes of Israel? What is a king of Sicily to an apostle of Christ? A wonderful man has risen up in our own, as we call it, wonderful time, — risen up from a moderate station to the empire of Europe; and yet the eight volumes which another wonderful man has written of that emperor's deeds and fortunes have not preserved, and cannot preserve, such a name for his hero as is secured by hardly more than eight lines, which tell us of those men who first fished for their living on the sea of Galilee, and then were called to be apostles of Christ.

My digression has led me far away, over distant countries and through many years. Let us return to the land of Judæa, and the history of

James. We ascertain that, among the twelve, he was one of those who were the most honored by the confidence of Jesus. With his former partner Simon, and his brother John, he was selected, as we have already seen, to accompany his Lord on several very important occasions; such as that of the resurrection of Jairus's daughter, the transfiguration, and the agony in the garden. It was perhaps on the strength of this manifest confidence, and of her own services, that Salome, the mother of James and John, made that ambitious and truly maternal request to Jesus, that her sons might sit on his right and left hand in his kingdom; that is, enjoy the two highest dignities next to his own, when he, as the Messiah, should mount the throne of Israel.

This is another instance of the universal misapprehension which then prevailed, and from which the disciples of Jesus were not free, concerning the office of the expected Messiah. It was with a complete understanding of this misapprehension, that Jesus now answered the deceived and partial mother: "Ye know not what ye ask. Are ye able to drink of the cup that I shall drink of, and to be baptized with the baptism that I am baptized with? Will you partake wholly of my lot? will you be able to adhere to me through every adversity, and share all my toils and dangers with me?" The brothers, whom in reality Jesus addressed, and through whose instigation it was that their mother had spoken to him, now answered him, under the persuasion that they could readily undergo a few trials in his service, in order to be at length advanced to great dignity under him, "We are able." How full of melancholy meaning is the reply of our Saviour! "Ye shall drink indeed of my cup, ye shall drain its full measure of sufferings to the dregs; and be baptized with the baptism that I am baptized with, even the waters of violent death; but to sit on my right hand and on my left, to prescribe your rank and degree in this world or the next, is not mine to give; it shall be given to those for whom it is prepared of my Father." As soon as the other disciples heard of the ambitious application of the sons of Zebedee, they were moved with indignation against them; but their Master, to quell their rising jealousy and ill-will, told them that the princes of the Gentiles, merely temporal governors, did indeed exercise that authority which they were so anxious to possess; but that it should not be so among them, but that they who would be great, truly great, among them, should minister the most kindly to each other's wishes and necessities; for in his kingdom that man would be chief in estimation and place, who was chief in benevolence, usefulness, and virtue.

The brothers are again exhibited to us in no very amiable light. We read in the ninth chapter of the Gospel of Luke, that, when the time approached in which Jesus was to finish his mission on earth, he set out to go from Galilee to Jerusalem; and as his way led through Samaria, he sent messengers before him to a Samaritan village, to prepare for his hospitable reception. The Samaritans, knowing that he was going up to the feast of the Passover, and piqued that he should pass by their own temple, which was the rival of that of Jerusalem, would not receive him. The anger of James and John was kindled by this rudeness, and they said to Jesus, " Lord, wilt thou that we command fire to come down from heaven, and consume them, even as Elias did? But he turned and rebuked them, and said, Ye know not what manner of spirit ye are of. For the Son of man is not come to destroy men's lives, but to save them." The evangelist adds, in words simply descriptive of our Saviour's gentleness and forbearance, " And they went to another village."

We may collect, from these notices, that James was disposed to be ambitious and passionate; somewhat resembling Peter in these respects, as also in his real attachment to his Master. We can with difficulty suppose that his brother John heartily joined him on the above-mentioned occasions, because his character, as we shall see hereafter, was of a very gentle order; and therefore it is probable that he was prevailed upon by the more vehement and energetic James to concur in his sentiments and projects at those times. It can hardly be regretted, however, that these exposures of human infirmity took place, when we advert to the excellent precepts on the subjects of ambition and revenge which they drew from the Saviour. And it is likewise to be observed, that, with all his gentleness, John had a great deal of zeal, and, before that zeal was chastened by the influence and example of his Master, might have often displayed it without knowledge. Beside which, we not unfrequently see that the gentlest and most amiable have the keenest sense of injustice, and that, when they are roused to indignation, they are greatly roused. It may have been so with John. At any rate, he shared with his brother in the appellation of Boanerges, or Sons of Thunder, which Mark, in his catalogue of the twelve, informs us was the surname bestowed on them by Jesus, and which seems to have reference to the heat of their temper; though by some interpreters it is supposed to signify their powers of eloquence.

In the Book of Acts we hear of James but once, after his name is given in the enumeration of the eleven apostles; and then it is to hear of his death. "Herod the king stretched forth his hand to vex certain of the Church; and he killed James, the brother of John, with the sword." This Herod was Herod Agrippa, the grandson of Herod the Great, in whose reign Christ was born. He was a distinguished favorite of the Roman emperors, Caligula and his successor Claudius, though a strict and zealous observer of the Jewish law. On entering upon his government, he was desirous of doing something to please the Jewish populace, and for that end began to persecute the infant Christian Church, selecting for a principal victim James, the brother of John. We are informed by Clemens Alexandrinus, that, as the apostle was led forth to the place of execution, the person who had accused him was so touched with the courage and constancy which he displayed, that he repented of what he had done, came and fell down at his feet, and earnestly begged pardon for what he had said against him. St. James tenderly raised him up, kissed him, and said to him, "Peace be to thee, my son, and the pardon of thy faults." At this, his former accuser publicly professed himself a Christian, and so both were beheaded at the same time. Not long after this martyrdom, Herod suffered a miserable death, as is related in Acts xii. 23, and more at large by Josephus in the nineteenth book of his Antiquities.*

* The three Herods are connected in an unenviable manner

JAMES THE GREATER.

Though not the first Christian martyr, James was the first of the apostles who suffered martyrdom; the first among the twelve, who, in fulfilment of that solemn prediction, was called to drink of the cup and be baptized with the baptism of their Master; the first who manifested to the world that it was beyond the power of death itself to shake their fidelity to him.* If he was not spared to labor much for the Church, he was soon permitted to edify it by his sufferings, and was called kindly and early to his reward in heaven.

He is the James who is called by the Spaniards St. James of Compostella, and honored as their patron saint. They receive with general faith a wild and singular legend, which gives an account of the manner in which they became possessed of his remains. According to this story, the apostles at Jerusalem sent the body in a ves-

---

with the early history of Christianity, each as a shedder of innocent blood. The first, Herod the Great, murdered the Innocents of Bethlehem; the second, Herod Antipas, beheaded John the Baptist; and the third slew James, and intended to have slain Peter. These circumstances are commemorated in the following Latin couplet: —

"Herodes Magnus pueros, Antipa Joannem,
Teque, Jacobe, Agrippa necat, Petrum et capit idem."

* He is therefore called the *Apostolic Protomartyr;* Stephen being the *Protomartyr,* or first martyr, of the whole Christian Church.

sel with Ctesiphon, whom they ordained bishop of Spain. The vessel went directly to a port in that kingdom, without the assistance of oars or pilot, guided only by its holy, though lifeless burden, which, on its arrival, was miraculously taken away and buried, and after a great many wonders, was at last translated to Compostella,* where it still abides, the object of constant pilgrimage, and the worker of countless miracles. Cave, after giving this legend rather more at length, observes: "This is the sum of the account, call it romance or history, which I do not desire to impose any further upon the reader's faith than he shall find himself disposed to believe it." It is a pity that such stories as this should be connected with the names of the holy apostles. It would be more a pity, however, if it were more difficult to separate legends from history, and falsehood from truth.

Ferdinand II. of Spain instituted a *military* order in honor of this apostle. His festival is on the 26th of July.

* It is said by some, that this place was first called Ad Jacobum Apostolum; then Giacomo Postolo; then, by contraction, Compostella.

JOHN.

WE now come to John, the brother of James the elder, and the last named, though certainly not the last in merit, of those four friends and partners, the fishermen of Bethsaida. The particulars of his call to be an apostle of Christ have already been related, together with some other circumstances respecting him, in the lives of Peter and James. We have seen that he ardently loved his Master; that he was distinguished by that Master's peculiar regard; and that, although he was sometimes betrayed into unworthy expressions of ambition and anger, for which he was justly reprimanded, his disposition was remarkably amiable, gentle, and affectionate.

There is not much told of him, individually, until towards the closing scenes of our Saviour's ministry and life. At the last supper, which he and Peter had been sent to prepare, we are told that "there was leaning on Jesus' bosom one of his disciples whom Jesus loved." This disciple was John himself; who was so fond of the distinction which his Master's attachment conferred on him, or, to speak more properly, was so gratefully sensible of the value of the attachment itself, that he continually speaks of himself, in his history, as the disciple whom Jesus loved, — a title which he surely would not have assumed unless it had been really conferred on him. His place at the supper is an evidence that he was high in the favor of Jesus. He was leaning or lying on his bosom; that is, he was the next below him, and, as it was the custom of the ancients to recline at their meals, his head was brought in contact with his Master's breast, — a situation which used always to be reserved by the host at an entertainment for the person whom he most honored or esteemed. It was while he was thus leaning, that Simon Peter beckoned to him that he should ask of Jesus who it was who should betray him. John did as he was requested, and Jesus showed him who the traitor was by giving Judas a sop. All this seems to have been done in private, and apart from the knowledge of the other disciples, and proves the great measure of condescension and confidence which was exercised by the Master toward this his favorite follower.

After Jesus was betrayed and seized, John is supposed to have been that other disciple who went with Peter to the palace of the high priest, and gained him admittance there by means of his acquaintance with that dignitary.* However this may be, he was the only one of the twelve who had the fortitude to attend his beloved Master to the cross. How touchingly is it manifested on this awful occasion, that the softest natures are often the noblest and most fearless too; and that those which are apparently the most daring and masculine may yet shrink away in the time of peril and distress! Who, in that hour of darkness, — darkness in the heavens and in the hearts of men, — who, in that hour of abandonment, when even the Son of God cried out that he was forsaken, — who, of all his followers, were with him then, to support him by their sympathy,

---

* "That disciple was known unto the high priest." John xviii. 15. The early writers busy themselves to find out in what manner John became acquainted with Caiaphas. Jerome says, that he belonged to some order of nobility; which, however, seems to be very inconsistent with the occupation of his father. Nicephorus relates, that he sold his paternal estate in Galilee to the high priest, and with the money purchased a fair house in Jerusalem, and so became intimate with him. These stories seem to me, like many other similar ones, to prove two things: one, that the early Christian writers were exceedingly anxious to explain the slightest hints in the Gospel histories; the other, that they were much too apt to write down the first report which came to their ears, glad to catch something, and not careful to sift the truth, or, rather, too ready to sacrifice truth to the gratification of a minute and inordinate, though not perhaps absolutely idle, curiosity. Hence the contradictory statements with which their works are full.

and prove to him their love? In the midst of scoffing soldiers and brutal executioners, under the lowering sky, and just below the frightful cross, we behold four weeping females,* and one disciple, the youngest and the gentlest of the twelve, braving the horrors of this place of blood, braving the anger of those in authority and the insults of those who do their bidding, determined to be near their friend and Master in his agonies, and ready, on the spot and at the moment, to share them. And what is it that braces up the nerves of this feeble company to such a singular pitch of fortitude and daring? The simple but unconquerable strength of affection; the generous omnipotence of their attachment and gratitude. In the might of their love they ascend the hill of Calvary, and take their station beneath the cross; hearing nothing amidst all that tumult but the promptings of their devoted hearts; seeing nothing but their dying Lord; remembering nothing but that he was dear to them, and that he was in misery. O, how loftily does courage like this rise above that ruder and earthly courage which rushes to the battle-field, and is crowned with

---

* They were Mary the mother of Jesus, Mary Magdalene, Mary the mother of James the Less and of Joses, and Salome the mother of James the Greater and of John. There were other women in company with them, but these four probably stood nearer the cross than the rest.

the applauses of the world! It calls for none of those excitements and stimulants from without which goad rough spirits into madness, but relies on those resources that are within, those precious stores and holy powers which are the strength of a single and faithful breast. That is the courage of the animal, this is of the soul. It is pure, it is divine. To say all in one word, it was such as moved the complacent regard of the Saviour himself, even in the height of his sufferings. Hanging on the cross, bleeding and exhausted, yet when he saw his mother, and the disciple standing by whom he loved, he was touched by their constancy; his thoughts were recalled to earth; the domestic affections rushed into his bosom; and with a tender care which provided at once a protection for his parent and a reward for his friend, "he saith unto his mother, Woman, behold thy son! Then saith he to the disciple, Behold thy mother!" Where was there ever so affecting a bequest as that which was then made, when love and filial piety triumphed over suffering? Where was there ever so affecting an adoption as that which then took place, when attachment and fidelity triumphed over fear? The last earthly care of Jesus was accomplished. His mother was confided to the disciple whom he best loved. The favorite disciple eagerly accepted the honorable and precious charge; for, "from that hour," as we are told by himself, he "took her unto his own home."

The whole scene is one of unrivalled pathos. Had it taken place in a quiet chamber, and by the side of a peaceful death-bed, it would have moved us; but how singularly and solemnly does it come in, a sweet and melting interlude, in the midst of that wild and appalling conflict, under the open and frowning heaven! It is like one of those hushed pauses between the fits of a midnight storm, when the elements wait, and pity seems pleading with wrath, ere the war and the turmoil begin again.

It would appear that the enemies of our Lord were satisfied, for that time, with his destruction; for we do not read that John, or the females who were with him, suffered any harm on account of their fearless exposure. It is probable also that the prodigies which succeeded the death of Jesus deterred his executioners from pursuing any further their work of blood.

On the morning of the resurrection, Mary Magdalene having gone to the sepulchre early, and observed that the stone was taken away from its mouth, announced this fact to Simon Peter and to John, who both ran toward the spot. John outran Peter, and came first to the sepulchre, and, stooping down, saw the linen clothes in which his Master had been buried; but he went not in.

Then Peter came up, and went in, and then John followed him. Why the latter did not go in immediately does not appear from the history; nor is it easy to form a conjecture; for he was certainly equal to Peter, both in courage and attachment to his Master. Perhaps in the mere agitation of his feelings he delayed till Peter arrived; who no sooner came up, than, with his characteristic promptness, he descended into the sepulchre where his crucified Lord had been deposited, in order, it may be, that he might ask forgiveness, even of his remains, for having so shamefully denied him.

A passage in John's own account of this visit to the tomb of Jesus renders it probable that he was the first person who believed in the resurrection of his Lord. "Then went in also that other disciple, who came first to the sepulchre, and he saw, and believed"; that is, believed that Jesus had arisen from the dead. Nor is this obvious interpretation contradicted by the succeeding verse: "For as yet they knew not the Scripture, that he must rise again from the dead." By the word "they" is not meant Peter and John particularly, but all the disciples. The belief was not yet received among them, that their Master was to rise from the dead; and therefore it was a remarkable circumstance, and one worthy of being recorded, that John was the first who remembered the predictions of Jesus, and acknowledged their fulfilment. So unprepared were the disciples for his resurrection, that Peter, who first saw that the tomb was empty, did not think of ascribing the fact to its true cause. It was into the mind of the beloved disciple that the light first broke. He first believed the glorious truth, that death was vanquished by the Son of God, and that Jesus of Nazareth was the Prince of Life.

When Jesus appeared to his disciples for the third time after his resurrection, and at the close of his solemn address to Peter intimated to him that he should die a violent death, that disciple, seeing John just behind, desired to know what his lot was to be. The answer of Jesus was, "If I will that he tarry till I come, what is that to thee?" This answer caused a saying to go abroad that John should not die; but we shall presently see what was the probable meaning of our Saviour's prophetic words.

In the Book of Acts we again meet with John in company with Peter, when the lame man was healed at the Beautiful Gate. This act of mercy and divine power occasioned their imprisonment. They were brought together before the council of priests and scribes; they were both charged to teach no more in the name of Jesus; they both nobly refused to obey; and they were both dismissed by the council, who were afraid at that time to punish them. It is pleasing to see those who had formerly been partners in a lowly but honest calling, thus continuing to toil hand in hand, in their more exalted profession of fishers of men. It is an exhibition of Christian friendship which should not pass unnoticed. On one other occasion they were united in their holy labors, when they were sent by the apostles on the mission to Samaria; after which we hear no more of John in the historical portion of the Scriptures.

All early testimonies agree, however, that he was spared to a great age, and outlived all the apostles; earnestly occupied, while his strength remained, in the service of his Master and the promotion of his religion. It is said by some writers that he preached to the Parthians; and it is certain that he dwelt for some time at Ephesus, where Mary, his adopted mother, whom he had constantly taken care of, according to the solemn testament of her own son, is supposed by some to have ended her days. It is more probable, however, as expressly stated by Eusebius, that she died before John left Judæa, about fifteen years after the Ascension of Jesus.

In the year of our Lord 70, and when John was about seventy years of age, the destruction of Jerusalem, by Titus, took place. It is understood by commentators generally, that it was this event to which Jesus referred, when he intimated that John should tarry till his coming. If so, the prediction was remarkably fulfilled; for this disciple was the only one of the twelve who lived to see that once proud city utterly overthrown, her glorious temple destroyed, and the very ground on which it stood ploughed up by the hands of heathen.

Between the years 90 and 100, and in the reign of the Emperor Domitian, he was banished to the Isle of Patmos, in the Ægean Sea. Here he wrote the Book of the Revelation; and here he remained till the death of Domitian, whose successor, Nerva, recalled those who had been banished for their faith in the preceding reign. He then returned to Ephesus, where he is said to have written his Gospel, and where he died a natural and peaceful death, at the extreme old age of one hundred years. According to Epiphanius, he died at the age of ninety-four, in the one hundredth year of the Christian era; a calculation which makes him six years younger than our Lord. But others say that he lived to the age which was first mentioned; and others again assert that his life was protracted beyond that term. All agree, however, that he was more than ninety at his death. He was spared to bear the longest, as his brother James was called to bear the earliest witness, of all the apostles, to the truth of Christ.*

He left several writings behind him, which have been preserved in the Church from age to age, and which of themselves bear witness to the affectionate mildness of his character. His Gospel was written after the three others; which accounts for its omitting many things which they relate, and relating many things which they omit. It is John alone who tells us of the resurrection of Lazarus; of Christ's washing his disciples' feet; and especially of those divine discourses which he held with them just before he was betrayed, and which were treasured up in the faithful memory and kindred heart of the beloved disciple, with a minuteness which proves how deeply he had been impressed by them.

The Book of the Revelation, which antiquity also ascribes to John, though not with an entirely unanimous voice, has both exercised and baffled as much critical ingenuity and research as ever were bestowed on any writing in the world. The majority of its interpreters have regarded it as a series of particular prophecies; and these sup-

* So respectable a writer as Chrysostom asserts, in one of his sermons, that John was an hundred years old when he wrote his Gospel, and that he lived twenty years afterwards. But this is worthy of but little credit. Again, many of the ancients entertained the notion that this apostle never died, but was translated, like Enoch and Elias.

posed prophecies have been applied to so many events, past 'and to come, that the reader is at last convinced that the truth does not even lie between the differing hypotheses. It may be that its splendid visions are really of a prophetic nature, and that they are not yet accomplished. But perhaps the most rational theory is that which several learned men have adopted, and which supposes that the whole Book of the Revelation is a general prediction, in the form of a religious drama, of the glorious success of Christianity in the world, and its triumph over its numerous foes, without any reference to the political condition of certain states and empires, or to the downfall of particular hierarchies or heresies. This opinion has been explained and supported by the German professor, Eichorn, in a commentary on the Revelation; and in earlier times had been maintained by able expositors, and espoused by no less a man than the poet Milton, who thus speaks in his *Reason of Church Government urged against Prelaty.* "And the Apocalypse of St. John is the majestic image of a high and stately tragedy, shutting up and intermingling her solemn scenes and acts with a sevenfold chorus of hallelujahs and harping symphonies; and this my opinion, the grave authority of Pareus, commenting that book, is sufficient to confirm." But whatever difference there may be concerning the intention of this book, there can be none with regard to its composition. It is undoubtedly a magnificent specimen of holy poetry; and reminds us more constantly and strongly of the sublimest of the Jewish prophecies than any other book in the canon of the New Testament.

Beside the two works already named, we have three epistles appearing in the Christian Scriptures as the productions of the Apostle John. That he wrote the one which is called the first, there has never been any dispute; it is universally and by the best authorities ascribed to him. But the genuineness of the two others was questioned at a very early period; though the balance in their favor appeared so great, that they were admitted into our present collection of sacred books. The controversy need not trouble us, however, as the two latter epistles, beside being very short, contain nothing of consequence which is not likewise contained in substance, and almost precisely in expression, in the first. This first epistle exhibits in a more striking light than do the rest of his writings his great amiableness of disposition. It is throughout an exhortation — an exhortation from the heart and soul and mind and strength of the writer — to pure, exalted, Christian benevolence; and its whole drift and spirit may be expressed in this single passage from the fourth chapter: " God is love; and he that dwelleth in love dwelleth in God, and God in him."

His merits as a writer are sententiously expressed in a passage from Jerome, who says, that " he was at once Apostle, Evangelist, and Prophet; — Apostle, in that he wrote letters to the Churches, as a master; Evangelist, as he wrote a book of the Gospel which no other of the twelve apostles did, except St. Matthew; Prophet, as he saw the revelation in the island of Patmos, where he was banished by Domitian. His Gospel, too, differs from the rest. Like an eagle he ascends to the very throne of God, and says, In the beginning was the Word."

To John, as well as to most of the apostles of Christ, are attributed by antiquity both writings and actions which are probably apocryphal and fabulous. It would be useless for me even to give the titles of the former. Of the traditions of his actions and miracles, one of the most generally known and quoted is the story that, during the persecution under Domitian, and just before the exile of John to Patmos, he was brought to Rome, and there thrown in a caldron of boiling oil, from which he came out altogether unhurt. In the pictures of him by the old painters, he is often represented as holding a cup or goblet, from which a serpent is rearing its head. This accompaniment refers to another legend respecting him, by one Prochorus, who tells us that, some heretics having presented the apostle with a cup of poisoned liquor, he made the sign of the cross over it, and all the venom was immediately expelled from the vessel, embodied in the visible form of a serpent.*

Stories of this kind would naturally be multiplied in that, or indeed in any age, concerning persons whose lives were singularly out of the common course, and who were in reality gifted with the power of working miracles. The ancient writers and fathers were too apt to promulgate such legends, without distinguishing them, as carefully as they ought to have done, from accounts which were worthy of credit; and the Church, finding how ready and even eager the multitude were to receive every tale of wonder, made it a part of its policy to cherish their credulity and strengthen their delusion. But we, who are of a more simple taste, require no such means to interest us in the history of a person in every way so interesting as the "disciple whom Jesus loved."

One of the best authenticated stories of his

* There is also generally introduced in the pictures of this saint the figure of an eagle. This is because he is supposed to be mentioned in the Book of the Revelation as the last of the "four beasts" near the throne, who was "like a flying eagle." We have seen above, also, that Jerome compares him to an eagle.

latter days, which is further recommended by its conformity with the known gentleness and amiableness of his character, cannot but please all readers, and I will therefore insert it. It is said that when the infirmities of age so grew upon him at Ephesus, that he was no longer able to preach to his converts, he used, at every public meeting, to be led to the church, and say no more to them than these words, "Little children, love one another." And when his auditors, wearied with the constant repetition of the same thing, asked him why he always said this and nothing more to them, he answered: "Because it was the command of our Lord; and that if they did nothing else, this alone was enough."

"Such," says Dr. Watts, in one of his sermons, — "such was John the beloved disciple. You may read the temper of his soul in his epistles. What a spirit of love breathes in every line! What compassion and tenderness to the babes in Christ! What condescending affection to the young men, and hearty good-will to the fathers, who were then his equals in age! With what obliging language does he treat the beloved Gaius, in his third letter; and with how much civility and hearty kindness does he address the elect lady and her children, in the second! In his younger years, indeed, he seems to have had something more of fire and vehemence, for which he was surnamed

A son of thunder. But our Lord saw so much good temper in him, mixed with that sprightliness and zeal, that he expressed much pleasure in his company, and favored him with peculiar honors and endearments above the rest. This is the disciple who was taken into the holy mount with James and Peter, and saw our Lord glorified before the time. This is the disciple who leaned on his bosom at the holy supper, and was indulged in the utmost freedom of conversation with his Lord. This is the man who obtained this glorious title, ' The disciple whom Jesus loved'; that is, with a distinguishing and particular love. As a Saviour he loved them all like saints, but as a man he loved St. John like a friend; and when hanging upon the cross, and just expiring, he committed his mother to his care, — a most precious and convincing pledge of special friendship.

"O how happy are the persons who most nearly resemble this apostle, who are thus privileged, thus divinely blessed! How infinitely are ye indebted to God, your benefactor and your Father, who has endowed you with so many valuable accomplishments on earth, and assures you of the happiness of heaven! It is he who has made you fair or wise; it is he who has given you ingenuity, or riches, or perhaps has favored you with all these; and yet has weaned your hearts from the love of this world, and led you to the pursuit of eternal life. It is he that has cast you in so refined a mould, and given you so sweet a disposition; that has inclined you to sobriety and every virtue, has raised you to honor and esteem, has made you possessor of all that is desirable in this life, and appointed you a nobler inheritance in that which is to come. What thankfulness does every power of your natures owe to your God! that Heaven looks down upon you and loves you, and the world around you fix their eyes upon you and love you; that God has formed you in so bright a resemblance of his own Son, his first-beloved, and has ordained you joint heirs of heaven with him."

Besides the affectionate title which so peculiarly connects this disciple with his Master, he is styled by ancient writers, "John the Divine," on account of the sublimity and spirituality of his writings.

His day is December 27 in the Roman Calendar; but the Greeks keep it on the 26th of September. And it may here be observed, that the Roman and Greek Calendars differ from each other in their dates throughout the ecclesiastical year.

PHILIP.

THE fifth named on Matthew's catalogue of the apostles is Philip. He was a native of Bethsaida, and consequently a townsman of the four partners whose histories I have already told. "Now Philip was of Bethsaida, the city of Andrew and Peter." We have no certain intelligence of his parentage or condition, though he was probably in the same rank of life with Peter and Andrew, James and John, and perhaps of the same profession.

The day after Peter and Andrew had become disciples of Christ, we read that "Jesus would go forth into Galilee, and findeth Philip, and saith unto him, Follow me." Though Peter and Andrew were the first who appear to have attended on the instructions of Jesus, and to have been particularly noticed by him, and are therefore termed his first disciples,—and though Andrew is styled *Protocletos*, as having been the first, whose name we know, who was invited to visit him and converse with him,—it is certain that the distinction belongs to Philip of having been the first who received that express and authoritative call to the apostleship, "Follow me." We find this account in the latter portion of the first chapter of John's Gospel. And we then read, further, that " Philip findeth Nathanael, and saith unto him, We have found him of whom Moses in the law, and the prophets, did write, Jesus of Nazareth, the son of Joseph." His conduct in this instance is like that of Andrew, as he manifested the same readiness to acknowledge Jesus as the Messiah, and the same zeal to make known his discovery to others.

This faith and zeal, however, do not continue to be, if we may judge from what little the Gospels relate of Philip, so firm and ardent afterwards as they seem to have been at first. When Jesus, in order to prove him, asked him where bread enough could be bought to feed the five thousand who were gathered together on the mountain, Philip, either not remembering the miraculous power of his Master, or not yet fully convinced of its reality, entered into a calculation, and returned, for answer, that two hundred pennyworth of bread would not be sufficient to supply every one with a little. And at the last supper, when our Lord was discoursing so divinely to his disciples, and had said to them, that, if they had known him properly, they would have known his Father, whom very soon they would both know and see,

Philip was so entirely unconscious of his meaning, and so blind, notwithstanding his long intimacy with Jesus, — so blind to the presence and agency of God in this, his beloved Son, — as to say to his Master, "Lord, show us the Father, and it sufficeth us." Grieved at his dulness and insensibility, Jesus returns that sadly reproachful answer, "Have I been so long time with you, and yet hast thou not known me, Philip? He that hath seen me hath seen the Father; and how sayest thou then, Show us the Father? Believest thou not that I am in the Father, and the Father in me? The words that I speak unto you, I speak not of myself; but the Father that dwelleth in me, he doeth the works." As if he had said, Is it not evident to you that the power which you have seen me exert is more than human power? that the wisdom which you have so long been hearing from my lips is more than human wisdom? that the Father must have been with me, and in me, all this time, or I could not have thus acted and spoken? How can you then, who have been one of my constant companions, how can you say, Show us the Father? As a Jew, you certainly do not expect to see God in person; and how can you behold a brighter manifestation of his image and attributes than that which you have so long beheld in me? You do not know me, Philip, neither me nor my Father.

This instance of the apostle's incredulity and slowness of apprehension does not prove that he was more incredulous and dull than his brethren; it only shows how small the impression was which the extraordinary instructions and actions of Jesus had as yet produced on the whole twelve. They entered into his service with the Jewish ideas of a Messiah; and now, when he was just about to leave them, they were almost as ignorant of the spirituality of his kingdom as when they first joined themselves to him.

Nothing further is said in the sacred histories to assist us in elucidating Philip's character. The Book of Acts relates nothing concerning him; for we must not confound Philip the Apostle with Philip the Deacon or Philip the Evangelist, both of whom are there mentioned. The best ancient testimony specifies Scythia as the principal scene of his apostolical labors; from which country he came at last into Phrygia, and dwelt in Hierapolis, the chief city in the western part of that province.* There he preached the Gospel of his Master, and planted the seeds of faith in the midst of idolatry; and it is said by some, that it was by effecting the destruction of an object of superstitious worship that he incurred the hatred

---

* This city is mentioned by Paul, in his Epistle to the Colossians iv. 13. It was near to Colosse and Laodicea, and had probably been visited by Paul.

and persecution of a part of the inhabitants, who caused him to be imprisoned and severely scourged, and then hung by the neck to a pillar. By others, however, he is said to have died a natural death.

By a concurrence of authorities, Philip is stated to have been a married man, and to have had several daughters.

The festival of this apostle, according to the Calendar of the Western Church, is on the 1st of May.

BARTHOLOMEW.

THE next in order of the twelve is Bartholomew. Respecting him there is a still greater dearth of information than there is respecting Philip; for there is absolutely nothing told of him in the New Testament, unless we resort to the supposition, which many scholars have adopted, that he is the same person with Nathanael. In favor of this supposition there are several arguments, which form together a body of strong presumptive evidence.

It is observed, in the first place, that the Evangelists Matthew, Mark, and Luke, who all place Bartholomew on their catalogues of the apostles, never mention Nathanael; and that John, who gives the particulars of Nathanael's conversation with our Lord, never mentions Bartholomew. Secondly, as John acquaints us with the fact that Philip led *Nathanael* to Jesus, so, in the lists of the apostles by the other evangelists, Philip and *Bartholomew* are constantly joined together as companions. "As they were jointly called to the discipleship," says Cave, "so they are jointly referred to in the Apostolic Catalogue, as afterwards we find them joint companions in the writings of the Church." Thirdly, it is remarked that Nathanael is introduced, in the company of several apostles, in the twenty-first chapter of John's Gospel, in such a manner as to lead us to suppose that he likewise might be one. The passage is that which relates to the appearance of Jesus, after his resurrection, at the sea of Tiberias; on which occasion Peter swam to him from the vessel in which he and the rest were fishing. The disciples, who were present, are thus named: "There were together Simon Peter, and Thomas called Didymus, and Nathanael of Cana in Galilee, and the sons of Zebedee, and two other of his disciples." Fourthly, the difference in the two names, which may at first appear to be an argument against this supposition, is rather in its favor. Bartholomew signifies the son of Tolmai, just as Bartimeus, the blind man whom Jesus restored to sight, signifies the son of Timeus; *bar* being the Hebrew word for son. Nathanael, therefore, might have also been called Bartholomew, after his father, just as Simon was called Barjonas after his father. Bartholomew could hardly have been the only name of the apostle, because it is a patronymic; and when circumstances agree so well, why might not his first name have been Nathanael? That John never calls Nathanael by the other name of Bartholomew is no proof that he had no other name; for Matthew, though his other name was Levi, never calls himself by that name, throughout the whole of his own Gospel. And finally, we are led naturally to the presumption that Nathanael must have been an apostle, not only by the circumstance of his being named in the midst of four apostles, but by the tenor of the conversation which Jesus held with him, and the probability that he was one of the very earliest disciples.

If we are convinced by these considerations that Bartholomew was the same person with Nathanael, we of course know something of his character and history. We view him as an inhabitant of Cana, in Galilee, where was performed the first miracle of his Lord, soon after his interview with him; as probably called to be an apostle on the same day with Philip, by whom he was introduced to Jesus; and as one who was characterized by the Saviour, and therefore deservedly, as an "Israelite indeed, in whom there was no guile."

The guilelessness, candor, and honesty of Nathanael, or Bartholomew, were indeed strikingly exhibited in all the circumstances of that interview. Impressed with the idea of his countrymen, that Nazareth could not furnish any celebrated prophet, and surely not the Messiah, as soon as

Philip uttered the words, "Jesus of Nazareth, the son of Joseph," he exclaimed, "Can there any good thing come out of Nazareth?" But when Philip, very wisely, instead of arguing the point, simply said, "Come and see," he went at once, clearly perceiving the justice of the appeal, and determined to put his prejudice, or his opinion, to the only proper test of experiment. And when he had received a small, though to his mind sufficient, proof of the superior knowledge of Jesus, he gave in his adhesion on the spot, saying, "Rabbi, thou art the Son of God; thou art the king of Israel." Pleased with this readiness of conviction, the Saviour seems to have taken him from this moment into his confidence; for he promised him that he should "see greater things than these"; stronger proofs than the one just given of the divinity of his mission; wonders and testimonies so mighty and divine, that heaven would appear, as it were, "open, and the angels of God ascending and descending upon the Son of man."

Let our prepossessions and prejudices vanish as did those of Nathanael, as soon as they are touched by the beams of truth. Let us be sincere, simple, open-hearted, free from guile, as he was; "without partiality and without hypocrisy." To such a character belongs by inheritance the promise given to Nathanael. He who possesses it will see greater things day by day; he will be continually receiving brighter manifestations of truth and heaven.

> "The child like faith that asks not sight,
> Waits not for wonder or for sign,
> Believes, because it loves, aright,
> Shall see things greater, things divine.
>
> "Heaven on that gaze shall open wide,
> And brightest angels to and fro
> On messages of love shall glide
> 'Twixt God above and Christ below."

Nothing is particularly related concerning this apostle, by the sacred writers, beside what has been already adduced. By early ecclesiastical historians, he is said to have carried the Gospel as far as India, by which must be meant, as Cave thinks, the hither India, which was the country bordering upon the Asian Ethiopia, or Chaldea. Pantænus, a Christian philosopher of the latter part of the second century, and preceptor of Clemens of Alexandria, having travelled into Ethiopia, found there, as Eusebius relates, a copy of Matthew's Gospel in Hebrew, which had been left there by Bartholomew. Phrygia was also for a time the field of the apostle's labors, where he met with his former companion, Philip, and at the period of his martyrdom narrowly escaped crucifixion himself. Lastly, he came to Albanopolis in the greater Armenia, where he was persecuted, and finally crucified, on account of his efforts to overthrow the idolatry of the place. Some accounts speak of his having been flayed alive, previous to his crucifixion.

Legends and martyrologies affirm, what we need not believe, that his body removed from place to place, till it came at last to Rome, where it rested, and where it is now deposited, as Roman Catholics suppose, in a porphyry monument, under the Church of St. Bartholomew.

August the 24th is consecrated to him by the Western Church.

THOMAS.

THE seventh of the twelve is Thomas. In the Gospel of John he is styled "Thomas called Didymus," but everywhere else simply Thomas. It is probable that Didymus is merely an interpretation into Greek of the Hebrew word "Thomas," as they both mean *a twin*. And it may be that he really was what his name designates him to have been.* But we have no certain accounts whatever of his early life, nor of the early period of his apostleship.

The first mention which is made of him is on a most interesting occasion, and when he appears in a most interesting light. Shortly after our

---

* "It was customary," says Cave, "with the Jews, when travelling into foreign countries, or familiarly conversing with the Greeks and Romans, to assume to themselves a Greek or a Latin name, of great affinity, and sometimes of the very same signification, with that of their own country. Thus our Lord was called *Christ*, answering to his Hebrew title *Mashiach*, or the *Anointed*; *Simon* styled *Peter*, according to that of *Cephas*, which our Lord put upon him; *Tabitha* called *Dorcas*, both signifying a *goat*. Thus our *St. Thomas*, according to the Syriac importance of his name, had the title of *Didymus*, which signifies a *twin*; *Thomas*, which is called *Didymus*."

Lord had escaped from the hands of the Jews, who were about to stone him, and had gone away beyond Jordan, the sisters of Lazarus, his friend, sent to him, informing him that their brother was sick. Jesus remained two days, after hearing this intelligence, in the place where he was; for it was his intention, not to rescue, but to restore Lazarus from death, that God might be the more glorified; and then he said to his disciples, "Let us go into Judæa again." His disciples earnestly sought to dissuade him from this, as they thought it, rash determination, and said unto him, "Master, the Jews of late sought to stone thee; and goest thou thither again?" In answer to this expostulation, Jesus tells them, in figurative speech, that what he had to do must be done in its due season, and before the appropriate time was past; and then he adds, "Our friend Lazarus sleepeth; but I go that I may awake him out of sleep." The disciples, understanding him literally, answer, that if Lazarus was sleeping, he would recover, and therefore it was unnecessary to incur danger, merely for the sake of seeing him. "Then said Jesus unto them, plainly, Lazarus is dead. And I am glad for your sakes that I was not there, to the intent ye may believe; nevertheless, let us go unto him." It is at this crisis, when the apostles seem to be hesitating between the sense of imminent danger and the feeling of duty to their Master, the one holding them back, and the other urging them forward, that Thomas advances, faithful, bold, and with a mind made up to abide by Jesus at all hazards, and says unto his fellow-disciples, "Let us also go, that we may die with him." His intrepidity in this case had its effect, no doubt, on his brethren; for they all went to Bethany, the village of Lazarus, which was only about two miles from Jerusalem; and the result was one of the most remarkable and important miracles of our Lord; which was soon followed indeed, as the disciples had feared, and as he had foreseen, by his own violent death.

Thomas is again introduced as one of the speakers on the night of the last supper. As Jesus was discoursing to his disciples, endeavoring to prepare them for his approaching departure, and to lead them to the sublime and consoling truths of immortality, he said to them, "Whither I go ye know, and the way ye know." Thomas, who no more than the rest could believe that the Messiah was to die, and to be taken from the world, before he had achieved his expected glories and the deliverance of Israel, said to him, "Lord, we know not whither thou goest; and how can we know the way?" His thoughts had not accompanied his Master's thoughts; they were yet on the earth, groping about there after a destination and a path, though Jesus was pointing so plainly to the mansions of another world, and the true and spiritual way which led to them. And it was immediately afterwards that Philip, too, uttered those words of ignorance which we have just now considered, and which show how much that light was needed which was soon to break in upon them all.

Once more we hear of Thomas, in a manner which marks his character with some strong lines, and particularly distinguishes his life. On the evening of the resurrection, our Saviour came and stood in the midst of the disciples, and showed them the wounds in his hands and side, and satisfied them that he was indeed risen from the dead. But Thomas was not then with them, and when they told him that they had seen the Lord, he replied, that unless he not only should see those wounds, but be allowed also to touch them and put his hand in them, he would not believe.

There is a boldness and even obstinacy in this resolution, which at first is apt to offend us; but on reflection we may find that it was neither harsh nor unreasonable. He could not have refused his belief as he did, through a want of respect or affection for his Master; because he had but a short time before expressed his readiness to die with him. Neither did he hold in too slight regard the testimony of his brethren, considering the circumstances; for it was no common matter to which they testified; in almost any other case he would have believed their report, or the report of a single one of their number, but now the event which they related was too marvellous in itself, one too momentous in its consequences, to be received on the witness of men who might not wish to deceive, but who nevertheless might themselves be deceived or mistaken; and he would trust to nothing but his own senses to bring him decisive evidence of an occurrence on which the direction of his whole future life depended.

He thought too, no doubt, that he ought to be satisfied of this wonderful fact as well as the rest of the disciples, and in the same way; and he was unquestionably right in so thinking. If he was hereafter to journey through the world, teaching and asserting, with all his powers, and in the face of every peril, the resurrection of Jesus the Christ, it was needful that he should possess a deep conviction of the reality of that event, — such a conviction as, in the capacity of a companion, friend, pupil, and apostle of Jesus, he ought to have, and such a conviction as the world would surely require of him. The miracle had just occurred, as his brethren told him; if so, why should not he, standing in the same situation as they did, and to whom its truth was as important as to them,—why should not he have the same evidence as they did; nay, why should he not have more? Why should he not, not only on his own account, but as their representative, demand the opportunity of clearing away every shadow of doubt which might rest on so splendid a truth, both by seeing his risen Lord as they had, and touching him with his hands as they had not?

If we regard the incredulity of Thomas in this light, we shall see nothing improper in it, and shall be disposed to grant that it was no greater than, in his situation, was natural and justifiable. In this conclusion we are countenanced by the conduct of our Saviour himself, who neither refuses to show himself to his doubting disciple, nor manifests any displeasure at his freedom or his unbelief; for the narration of the occurrence is thus continued by St. John : " And after eight days, again his disciples were within, and Thomas with them. Then came Jesus, the doors being shut, and stood in the midst, and said, Peace be unto you. Then saith he to Thomas, Reach hither thy finger, and behold my hands; and reach hither thy hand, and thrust it into my side ; and be not faithless but believing." Startled, doubtless, by the sudden appearance of his Master, and affected too by the kind and assuring manner in which he is bid to satisfy his doubts completely, Thomas broke out into the exclamation of wonder and acknowledgment, "My Lord and my God!" His doubts were entirely overcome, his faith was now as ardent and lively as before his distrust had been cold; and his testimony to the reality of the resurrection is perhaps more valuable than any other single testimony, because it was rendered under such peculiar circumstances, and by one so honest and so sturdy in avowing his scruples, and so candid in resigning them. "By touching, in Christ," says one of the Fathers, "the wounds of the flesh, he has healed, in us, the wounds of unbelief."

The exclamation of Thomas, quoted above, has held so conspicuous a place, and been so often brought forward in theological controversy, that I must necessarily dwell for a moment on the consideration of its import. By many, though by no means by all of those who hold the doctrine of the perfect equality of the Son with the Father, it has been adduced as a Scripture proof of that equality; as an acknowledgment by the apostle of the Godhead and supreme divinity of Jesus Christ. To this interpretation of the passage, there seem to me to be insurmountable objections. In the first place, the question of the Deity of Christ has no concern with the event. It was not to be satisfied of the Deity, but of the resurrection of his Master, that Thomas required his appearance; and it was to convince him of that resurrection that his Master condescended to appear to him. "Except I shall see in his hands the print of the nails, and put my finger into the print of the nails, and thrust my hand into his side, I will not believe." Believe what? What the disciples had just told him, certainly, that they had seen the Lord, that he was truly alive, not that he was truly God. Secondly, it is difficult to conceive how the appearance of Jesus in a human form, just as he had always appeared before, and with bodily wounds, just as he had been taken from the cross, that is, as a man in all respects, could have convinced his disciple, and that disciple a Jew, that he was the eternal God. The miracle of the resurrection itself could not have had this effect, because Thomas had often witnessed the miracles of his Master, without once confessing that he was God; and no other evidence was at this time offered. Thirdly, if Jesus was on this occasion acknowledged to be God, it might be expected that the writer of the narrative should take some notice of the circumstance; but what are his words, immediately after relating this event? "These are written, that ye might believe that Jesus is *the Christ, the Son of God*"; not God himself. Fourthly, the exclamation itself is abrupt, and without any connection to de-

termine precisely its meaning. It might not have been addressed to Jesus at all, but to God alone; or the first appellation might have been addressed to him, and the second to Heaven; it was an exclamation, in short, of wonder, of ecstatic wonder, of ecstatic gratitude, and just such a one as any of us would be likely to utter on witnessing a similar marvel; such, for instance, as the resurrection of a dear friend from the grave. Fifthly, if the whole exclamation was really addressed to Jesus, the term God might well have been applied, according to known Jewish usage, and in its lower sense, to one who now had manifested undeniably that he was the Messiah, the Prince of Peace, the Son of God, and the King of Israel. Lastly, the answer of Jesus himself excludes the supposition that he was addressed as the Supreme God. For he said unto his disciple, "Thomas, because thou hast seen me thou hast believed; blessed are they that have not seen, and yet have believed." Now this must mean, "Because thou hast seen me here alive, after my crucifixion and burial, thou hast believed that I am raised from the dead; and it is well; but blessed are they who cannot have such evidence of the senses, and yet shall believe in the glorious truth, from your evidence, and that of your brethren." He could not have meant that they were blessed, who, though they had not seen him, yet had believed that he was God; because there is no connection between the propositions; because the fact of the resurrection of Jesus cannot, to the mind of any one, be of itself a proof of his Deity; and because no one thinks of requiring to see God, in order to believe that he exists. In conclusion, it must be remembered, that these considerations are so obvious that they have been fully adopted by some of those who still have professed their belief, founded on other evidence, of the Deity of Christ.

It cannot be doubted that the decided and resolute character of Thomas fitted him eminently for his apostolic duties. But the accounts which we have of his life and works after the ascension of his Master, though sufficiently copious, are too contradictory to claim our entire confidence. Some general facts, however, seem to be well established, and they are of an exceedingly interesting character. There is no good reason to doubt that this apostle penetrated as far into the East with his heavenly mission as to the Coromandel and Malabar Coasts of Indostan, and even to Taprobane, or Ceylon, visiting and preaching in other countries by the way. On those coasts he made a great number of converts, the descendants of whom, still professing Christianity, exist in that part of India at the present day, and are called the *St. Thomas Christians*, according to the testimony of Dr. Buchanan, Bishop Heber, and other enlightened travellers. This is a remarkable confirmation of the general statements of early ecclesiastical writers; and is a proof that we may receive many of their principal facts, without relying on their minute details or marvellous legends. These Christians of St. Thomas were known to the Western world in early times, but appear to have been lost sight of afterwards, till they were again discovered by navigators at the commencement of the sixteenth century. The see of Rome endeavored to bring them under its subjection, but with only partial success. A part of them are now Roman Catholics, but the majority form a church entirely independent of the Church of Rome. They possess the New Testament in the Syriac language.

The martyrdom of Thomas is stated to have taken place at Malipur or Meliapor, on the Coromandel coast, nor far from the present city of Madras, where he had converted the king of the country and many of his subjects, and had built a church. The Brahmins were enraged at his success, and by one of them he was run through the body with a lance, while he was kneeling at his devotions before a tomb. He was buried in the church which he had built; but his bones are said to have been afterwards translated to Edessa in Mesopotamia.

The following narrative by Bishop Heber, touching these events in the life of St. Thomas, is taken from his Journal in India, Vol. III. pages 212–214:—

"We went in a carriage to the military station of St. Thomas's Mount, eight miles from Madras, intending, in our way, to visit the spot marked out by tradition as the place where the Apostle St. Thomas was martyred. Unfortunately the 'Little Mount,' as this is called (being a small rocky knoll with a Roman Catholic church on it, close to Marmalong Bridge in the suburb of Meilapoor), is so insignificant, and so much nearer Madras than we had been given to understand, that it did not attract our attention until too late. That it really is the place, I see no good reason for doubting; there is as fair historical evidence as the case requires, that St. Thomas preached the Gospel in India, and was martyred at a place named Milliapoor or Meilapoor. The Eastern Christians, whom the Portuguese found in India, all agreed in marking out this as the spot, and in saying that the bones, originally buried here, had been carried away as relics to Syria. They and even the surrounding heathen appear to have always venerated the spot, as these last still do, and to have offered gifts here on the supposed anniversary of his martyrdom. And as the story contains nothing improbable from beginning to end (except a trumpery fabrication of some relics found here by the Portuguese monks about a century and a half ago), so it is not easy to account for the origin of such a story among men of different religions, unless there were some foundation for it.

"I know it has been sometimes fancied that the person who planted Christianity in India was a Nestorian Bishop named Thomas, not St. Thomas the Apostle; but this rests, absolutely, on no foundation but a supposition, equally gratuitous and contrary to all early ecclesiastical history, that none of the apostles except St. Paul went far from Judæa. To this it is enough to answer, that we have no reason why they should not have done so; or why, while St. Paul went, or intended to go, to the shores of the further West, St. Thomas should not have been equally laborious and enterprising in an opposite direction. But that all the apostles, except the two St. Jameses, did really go forth to preach the Gospel in different parts of the world, as it was, *a priori*, to be expected, — that they did so we have the authority of Eusebius and the old Martyrologies, which is at least as good as the doubts of a later age, and which would be reckoned conclusive, if the question related to any point of civil history. Nor must it be forgotten that there were Jews settled in India at a very early period, to convert whom would naturally induce an apostle to think of coming hither; that the passage either from the Persian Gulf or the Red Sea is neither long nor difficult, and was then extremely common; and that it may be, therefore, as readily believed that St. Thomas was slain at Meilapoor, as that St. Paul was beheaded at Rome, or that Leonidas fell at Thermopylæ. Under these feelings, I left the spot behind with regret, and shall visit it, if I return to Madras, with a reverent, though, I hope, not a superstitious interest and curiosity.

"The Larger Mount, as it is called, of St. Thomas, is a much more striking spot, being an insulated cliff of granite, with an old church on the summit, the property of those Armenians who are united to the Church of Rome. It is also dedicated to St. Thomas, but (what greatly proves the authenticity of its rival) none of the sects of Christians or Hindoos consider it as having been in any remarkable manner graced by his presence or burial. It is a picturesque little building, and commands a fine view."

A legend is quoted by Cave, from Gregory of Tours, concerning the tomb of this apostle at Malipur, which, though deserving of no more credit than other legends of the same class, is pleasing to the imagination. A lamp, says the legend, hangs before his tomb, which burns perpetually, needing no oil, and undisturbed by the wind or any accident whatever. Possibly a gaseous fountain might once have existed there, which would be a sufficient origin for the story; or some deception may have been practised by the priests.

The 21st of December is St. Thomas's day in the Western Calendar.

MATTHEW.

MATTHEW places himself the eighth on his list, and styles himself "the Publican." This avowal of his profession is at once a proof of his humility and his good sense. He had the meekness to set himself down exactly what he was, notwithstanding the contempt which the confession might bring upon him; and he had the wisdom to perceive that there was no rank or occupation in life, however low, which could change the nature of true worth, or really disgrace an honest and virtuous man.

To the Jews, above all other people, *publican* was an odious name. There is a use of this word among us, a low and improper use, which has nothing to do with its true signification and its Scripture sense; for a publican does not mean, in the Gospels, an innkeeper, but a tax-gatherer, or a receiver of the tribute imposed by government. The Romans employed these receivers of tribute, or publicans, in all their provinces, and, among the rest, in Judæa. Now, to pay tribute was not only a constant acknowledgment and badge of subjection and servitude, but to the Jews it was something more galling still, because it wounded their religious as well as their political pride. It was a thought of pure, unmitigated bitterness, that the people of God should thus pass periodically under the hated yoke of idolaters, and, as they would call them in their haughty exclusiveness, barbarians. The office itself being thus detestable, it may be conceived how those persons must have been looked upon who held and exercised it.

There were two orders, however, among the publicans,—the receivers general, who had deputies under them, and these deputies themselves. The former were usually selected from the best classes of society; but the latter were reckoned ignoble and contemptible, even by the Gentiles, and were, as a body, vulgar, rapacious, and unmerciful. Some one asked Theocritus which was the most cruel of all beasts; and he answered, "Among the beasts of the wilderness, the bear and the lion; among the beasts of the city, the publican and the parasite." Of the higher order of publicans at Jerusalem one is probably mentioned in the Gospel of Luke, by the name of Zacchæus, who is there said to be "the chief among the publicans," and a rich man. Of the lower order were those who are so frequently classed in the Scriptures with sinners; and of this order was Matthew. They were all, high and low, for the reasons just given, regarded with abhorrence by the Jews, and treated as a profane and outcast set of people. "Let him be unto thee *as a heathen man and a publican*" is a phrase which expresses strongly the universal ban which was suspended over them. We are told that, though a publican might be a Jew, he was hardly recognized as such by his countrymen; that he was not allowed to enter the temple, nor give testimony in courts of justice; that the gifts, even, which his devotion might prompt him to offer, were rejected from the altar of Jehovah, as unclean and abominable.

Bearing these things in mind, we can now estimate the self-denial of the apostle, who, with a firm pen, could write himself down, "Matthew, *the Publican.*"

In the second chapter of Mark, he is said to be the son of Alpheus; but whether this Alpheus is the same with the father of James the Less, or another individual, is uncertain. His place of residence was in Capernaum, or somewhere near it, on the sea of Tiberias. Though he constantly calls himself Matthew, he is called Levi by the other evangelists; and it is for this reason that Levi and Matthew have been supposed by some celebrated scholars to be two different persons. But the circumstances of Matthew's call to be a disciple, as related in his own Gospel, are so precisely similar to those which attend the call of Levi, as related in the Gospels of Mark and Luke, that the predominant opinion has always been, that Matthew and Levi were only two names for one and the same person.

Though a publican, of an inferior rank, belonging to a class of men who were considered vile, and who generally deserved their reputation, Matthew was an upright and religious man; and there was *one* of his countrymen, if there were no more, who could separate the man from the profession, and fearlessly engage him for his companion and friend. It was he who saw him sitting in his place of business, or at the receipt of custom, as it is called, and said unto him, "Follow me."* These were words, which, from those lips, could not be uttered in vain; and the humble publican, who probably had before heard the discourses of Jesus, and heard them with admiration, and seen also some of the wonders which he had done, immediately arose and followed him.

---

* It appears from the relation of Mark, in the second chapter of his Gospel, that Matthew's official station was at the seaside, where he was sitting when Jesus called him. Commentators say that the particular duty of Matthew as a publican was to gather the customs of commodities which came by the sea of Galilee, and the tribute which passengers were to pay who went by water According to this statement, he was a toll-gatherer.

Our Saviour, after having called Matthew, went to his house; and there his new disciple prepared a supper for him; and many publicans and sinners, the former associates of Matthew, came and sat down with Jesus and his disciples. When some Pharisees, who were present, saw this, they said to the disciples, "Why eateth your Master with publicans and sinners? But when Jesus heard that, he said unto them, They who are whole need not a physician, but they who are sick. But go ye, and learn what that meaneth, I will have mercy, and not sacrifice; for I am not come to call the righteous, but sinners to repentance."

In both of these incidents, the spirit of Christianity and the character of its founder are conspicuous. The call of a publican to be a follower of Christ and a herald of his religion was a sign of the sublime superiority of the new faith, in its impartiality and mercy, over the bigotries of the old; and evinces the discernment and the independence of Jesus in selecting a worthy disciple from an order of men among whom common opinion had pronounced that there was no worth to be found. And in sitting down to eat — that greatest token of familiarity — in the house of this publican, and with a mixed company of reputed sinners, Jesus again manifests the universal benevolence of his temper and his doctrine. To the hypocritical Pharisees, it was indeed a strange and scandalous thing, that one who set up as the Messiah of Israel, and the purifier of its ordinances, should take a publican to be a pupil, and break-bread with other publicans and notorious sinners; but how well are their narrow prejudices and their supercilious and uncharitable self-righteousness rebuked by the steadfast reply of the Saviour! "The religion which I would inculcate," as the reply may be paraphrased, "embraces in its pure mercy the whole family of man; it draws no impassable line between the privileged and the profane; it leaves none to despair of Heaven's favor and acceptance. If ye are perfect, if ye are whole, my errand is not to you; go; go to your temple and perform your rites; but when there, study the meaning of that scripture, I will have mercy and not sacrifice. As for these, they are sick; they need a physician, and I must heal them; ye yourselves say that they are sinners, and why shall I not call them to repentance, and save them?"

With what has been now told from the Gospels concerning Matthew, we must rest contented; but even from these slight memorials we shall gain a highly favorable impression of his character. In his depressed condition as a publican, he seems to have learned the valuable lesson of humility; and thus to have become "almost a

Christian," before he was a follower of Christ. Among his vile companions, whom public obloquy had made yet more vile than their habits and their occupation would have made them, he was upright, honest, merciful, uncontaminated. His integrity appears doubly bright by contrast, amidst the dark examples and fearful temptations which were all around it like clouds; and his virtue, reared among quicksands and waves, proved, simply by its being and standing there, how very deeply and strongly its foundations were laid. It is further to be remarked, that though he was the writer of one of the Gospel histories, he says nothing more of himself than that he was called to follow Jesus, while he was sitting in his office, and that he afterwards entertained his Master at his house; and this latter circumstance he only mentions in order that he may introduce the answer of Jesus to the Pharisees. We could have no better evidence than this of his disinterestedness and modesty.

His Gospel is everywhere distinguished by plain good sense and manly simplicity. It was written, as some of the ancients say, fifteen years after the ascension of our Saviour, or, as others affirm, yet seven years earlier, or, according to yet others, at a considerably later period than the latest of these two dates, that is, about the year 60, or between 60 and 70 of our era, while Peter and Paul were preaching at Rome. Although some critics have advanced the opinion that Luke's Gospel was the first which was written, the general voice of antiquity is against them, and a majority also, I believe, of the moderns. So that the Gospel of Matthew really stands, in all probability, where a place is given to it in our Bibles, — the first in order of the four evangelical histories.

Another circumstance respecting this Gospel, which the earliest ecclesiastical authors record, and which, though it has been controverted, is most probably a fact, is, that we do not possess it in the language in which it was originally composed. It was written by Matthew, according to the best testimony, at Jerusalem, on purpose for the Jewish converts, and in that modern dialect or species of Hebrew which was the common language, at that time, of Palestine. The Gospel in that language has been lost, it is supposed, irretrievably. That which we have is a translation of it into Greek, made very soon after the original was composed. There is no reason to challenge its exact faithfulness to the original; and some have even supposed that Matthew himself was the author of this Greek rendering of his own Hebrew Gospel. The predominant opinion is, however, that the name of the translator, and the Gospel which he translated, are alike unknown and undiscoverable. Though we may be allowed to regret that we cannot look on the very words which this excellent apostle used in narrating, for our exceeding benefit, the life and actions of his Master, yet our faith ought not to be in the least disturbed by the loss, while there remains to us a translation of his history, so manifestly ancient, complete, and true.

I am well aware that there are great names to be brought against the commonly received opinions of the priority of Matthew's Gospel, and its having been originally written in Hebrew. There are also great names in favor of those opinions. And I confess I am somewhat surprised that the name of Lardner stands in the former class. Irenæus, on whose authority, as being the most ancient, he justly relies, expressly says that the Gospel was written in Hebrew; and though he seems to assign the latest of the three dates to its composition, he evidently means to leave the impression that it was written before the other Gospels. I will now give the passage from Irenæus — who wrote about the year 178 — precisely as it is given in Lardner's own immortal work.

"Matthew then among the Jews wrote a gospel in their own language, while Peter and Paul were preaching the gospel at Rome, and founding [or establishing] the church there. And after their exit [that is, death, or departure] Mark also, the disciple and interpreter of Peter, delivered to us, in writing, the things that had been preached by Peter. And Luke, the companion of Paul, put down in a book the gospel preached by him. Afterwards John the disciple of the Lord, who leaned upon his breast, likewise published a gospel, whilst he dwelt at Ephesus, in Asia."

And the next authority cited by Lardner is that of Origen, who says, about the year 230, " that according to the tradition received by him, the first gospel was written by Matthew, once a publican, afterwards a disciple of Jesus Christ; who delivered it to the Jewish believers, composed in the Hebrew language." To the same purpose is the testimony of Eusebius, the third cited authority.

Although Dr. Lardner's arguments against the Hebrew original of Matthew's Gospel are learned and ingenious, they cannot convince me in opposition to such authorities. And let it be observed, that the date assigned by Irenæus to its composition is not a fixed and certain date, because the period of the preaching of Peter and Paul at Rome is not a fixed or certain year. But the priority of the Gospel is a fixed and certain fact, according to that Father, and so is the language in which it was written.

Matthew is said to have carried the religion

of Jesus into Parthia and Ethiopia, and to have suffered martyrdom at Naddaber, in the latter country, but by what death is uncertain. We are told also that his remains were brought to Bithynia, and from thence to Salernum, in the kingdom of Naples, where they were discovered in the year 1080, and where a church was built for them by Duke Robert, in the pontificate of Gregory VII. We can readily believe that relics were thus found and honored, which were declared, and by many supposed, to be the body of the apostle; but that they really were so, we are at perfect liberty to question and to deny.

Matthew's festival is on the 21st of September.

JAMES THE LESS.

NEXT to his own name, Matthew writes that of "James, the son of Alpheus"; who is also called, in the Gospel of Mark, "James the Less," or the younger, to distinguish him from the other apostle of the same name, James the brother of John, who was older than he; or it may be that he was of small stature, and therefore named "the less."

His mother's name was Mary. She was one of the Marys who were present at the crucifixion of our Saviour; and appears to have been the sister of Mary the mother of Jesus. In the Gospel of Mark she is called "Mary, the mother of James the Less, and of Joses." In a parallel passage of John's Gospel, she is mentioned as follows: "There stood by the cross of Jesus, his mother, *and his mother's sister, Mary the wife of Cleophas*, and Mary Magdalene." From these passages the inference is justly drawn, that James the Less was the first cousin of Jesus. He is expressly called the son of Alpheus and of Mary; and as Mary, who was the wife of Alpheus, which is only the Greek pronunciation of the Hebrew name Cleophas, is also termed in the same passage the sister of our Lord's mother, he is consequently our Lord's cousin.

He is the same person who is mentioned by Paul, when he says, in his Epistle to the Galatians, "But other of the apostles saw I none, save James, the Lord's brother." To account for this appellation, it must be observed that the Jews were accustomed to include all near relations under the general name of brethren. And we may also remark, that, though it appears strange that Mary should be the sister of Mary, it was not uncommon among the Jews, that two sisters of the same family should bear the same name. James is likewise enumerated among the Lord's brethren by the Jews, when they asked in astonishment, "Is not this the carpenter's son? is not his mother called Mary? and his brethren, James, and Joses, and Simon, and Judas?" Of these four sons, three were apostles of Jesus; and the other one, Joses, or Joseph, was probably a disciple; as was Cleophas too, or Alpheus, the father of this Christian family.

The exact relationship to Jesus of James the Less, and others who are called his brethren, was a matter of controversy in very early times. Respectable names appear on each side; and Cave says that a majority of the ancients were of opinion that these "brethren" were actually the sons of Joseph by a former wife. It has appeared to me that the other opinion is the most likely to be the true one, and I have therefore called James the cousin of Jesus. One of the strongest arguments for this view of the relationship is, that the father of James is called Alpheus, and not Joseph, and that Mary the wife of Cleophas is mentioned in the Gospel of John as a person entirely distinct from the mother of Jesus, and further appears to be the same who is called by Mark the mother of James the Less and of Joses. Now Alpheus and Cleophas being the same name, the chain of testimony is complete, — so complete, that I wonder any question should ever have been raised on the subject. It may be added, that Lardner inclines to the opinion that James was cousin to our Lord.

No particulars are related of James in the Gospels; but honorable mention is made of him in the Book of Acts and the Epistles of Paul. Perhaps his youth and his modesty, together with his near relationship to Jesus, operated upon him to be silent and inactive during the life of the Saviour, though afterwards his talents and worth made him conspicuous. He appears to have resided constantly at Jerusalem, and to have been president or bishop of the church there. All antiquity affirms this, and Scripture gives it good countenance. Thus we are told in the twelfth chapter of Acts, that when Peter had been miraculously delivered from the prison into which he had been thrown by Herod, who had just slain the other James, he went to the house of a believing family, and said to those who were there, "Go, show these things unto James, and the brethren." James is evidently spoken of here as having a precedence among the brethren. Again, in the fifteenth chapter of the same book, he appears to have been the presiding member of the Council of Jerusalem, of which I have before had occasion to speak, and which decided that the Gentiles were to be received, on their conversion, into the full privileges of the Christian Church, without being obliged to undergo the ceremony of circumcision. It has been observed, that, though Peter spoke first on this occasion, James spoke last, and gave his opinion or "sentence" with regard to the most proper course to be pursued, and that the letter or result of the council was chiefly modelled upon his words. From these circumstances it has been concluded that he was the moderator or president of this first Christian council, and that this rank was probably conceded to him on account of his being the presiding apostle or bishop of Jerusalem, in which place the council was convened. Peter, as it may be remembered, agreed with James entirely in this case; but, though in some sense chief of the apostles, it is evident that when the Church came to be enlarged and settled, he did not possess any general supreme authority, but, as in the present council, was regarded, and regarded himself, as in subordination to the local authorities. The speech of James is replete with good sense, dignity, and a spirit of charity and forbearance, and sufficiently indicates the wisdom of his brethren in making him bishop or overseer of the Christian Church at Jerusalem.

In the twenty-first chapter of Acts there is also a particular mention of James, which corroborates the preceding proofs of his consequence in the Church. In an account there given of the journey of Paul and his company to Jerusalem, with the collections for the saints in Judæa, the writer says: "And when we were come to Jerusalem, the brethren received us gladly. And the day following, Paul went in with us unto James; and all the elders were present." James could hardly have been singled out by name in this passage, for any other reason than because he was the chief person at this convocation of the elders.

To all this evidence of the standing of James and the high consideration in which he was held, the testimony of Paul himself is to be added. One passage has already been adduced from the first chapter of his Epistle to the Galatians. In the second chapter, Paul says: " And when James, Cephas, and John, who seemed to be pillars, perceived the grace that was given unto me, they gave to me and Barnabas the right hands of fellowship, that we should go unto the heathen, and they unto the circumcision." Here it is to be noted that James is not only called one of the pillars of the Church, but is placed at the head of the three; even before Cephas, or Peter. At the same time we ought to observe that ecclesiastical rank was by no means, in those primitive times, that thing of name and pomp and prerogative that it has since been made in most of the churches of Christendom; for if James had been the bishop of Jerusalem in the same sense in which the title is now applied, Paul would never have said of him and the others, that they " seemed to be pillars,"— an expression which plainly signifies, that they appeared, as far as he could judge, to be the first men in the Church. In truth, a bishop in those days was only a moderator among brethren and equals, appointed to the office by them, and appointed to it for his superior gifts and attainments.

Once more, and in this same chapter, is James mentioned. Paul, in relating the vacillating conduct of Peter, with regard to eating with the Gentiles, says, in the words which I have already quoted in Peter's life: " Before that certain came from James, he did eat with the Gentiles; but when they were come, he withdrew and separated himself." Here again is James spoken of as a person of consideration and authority.

Thus far do the Scriptures inform us of the life and character of James the Less. Ancient ecclesiastical writers have much to say of his virtues and wisdom, and of the respect which they procured for him, both among the faithful and the unbelieving. The Jews, we are told, were unbounded in their admiration of him; insomuch that, as Jerome affirms, they used to strive to touch the hem of his garment. On account of his remarkable integrity, he obtained another surname beside that which is given to him in the Scriptures, and was called James the Just. Some go so far as to say, that he was allowed to enter into the Holy of Holies of the Jewish temple; but this must be a fiction. It is a fiction, however, which, together with other similar ones, shows that there must have been a foundation for them in the high character and reputation of this apostle.

The circumstances of his death are differently stated. Josephus, the Jewish historian, is supposed to relate it in the following passage from the twentieth book of his Antiquities, which I give in the translation of L'Estrange. "The Ananus we are now speaking of [who had recently been raised to the high-priesthood by Agrippa] was naturally fierce and hardy; by sect a Sadducee, the most censorious and uncharitable sort of people upon the face of the earth. This being his way and opinion, he took his opportunity, in the interval betwixt the death of Festus and the arrival of his successor Albinus, who was as yet but upon the way, to call a council together, with the assistance of the judges, and to cite James, the brother of Jesus, which was called Christ, with some others, to appear before them, and answer to a charge of blasphemy, and breach of the law; whereupon they were condemned, and delivered up to be stoned." The account proceeds to say that all the sober and conscientious part of the city were so much offended with this high-handed way of acting, that they sent a representation of it, with a remonstrance, both to King Agrippa and to Albinus; the consequence of which was, that Ananus was deposed by Agrippa from the pontificate. This passage would be decisive, were it not that several learned men question the genuineness of the words, " the brother of Jesus which was called Christ." Lardner thinks that they are an interpolation, and inclines to the account given by Eusebius, in the second book of his Ecclesiastical History ; who says, " When Paul had appealed to Cæsar, and had been sent to Rome by Festus, the Jews, who had aimed at his death, being disappointed in that design, turned their rage against James, the Lord's brother, who had been appointed by the apostles bishop of Jerusalem"; and then he goes on to state that James was killed in a popular tumult. If this narrative is the true one, it makes the death of the apostle a year or two earlier than it is dated by Josephus; but at any rate we may safely fix it somewhere about the year 60, and eight or ten years before the destruction of Jerusalem. He was buried, according to Gregory, bishop of Tours, on Mount Olivet, in a tomb which he had built for himself.

So great was the reputation of James for sanctity, that his death was supposed by the Jews themselves to have hastened the destruction of their city. Some of the Fathers tell us that this was asserted by Josephus; but the passage is not now to be found in his works. Both the accounts of James's death agree that he was stoned. It is added in the relation of Hegesippus, as preserved by Eusebius, that he was finally despatched by the blow of a fuller's club.

The following excellent summary of the main facts in the life of James is from the close of Lardner's account of that apostle.

"James, sometimes called the Less, the son of Alpheus, and called the Lord's brother, either as being the son of Joseph by a former wife, or a relation of his mother Mary, was one of Christ's apostles. We have no account of the time when he was called to the apostleship. Nor is there anything said of him particularly in the history of our Saviour which is in the Gospels. But from the Acts, and St. Paul's Epistles, we can perceive that after our Lord's ascension he was of note among the apostles. Soon after St. Stephen's death in the year 36, or thereabout, he seems to have been appointed president or superintendent in the church of Jerusalem, where, and in Judæa, he resided the remaining part of his life. Accordingly, he presided in the Council of Jerusalem, held there in the year 49 or 50. He was in great repute among the Jewish people, both believers and unbelievers, and was surnamed the Just. Notwithstanding which, he suffered martyrdom in a tumult at the temple; and probably in the former part of the year 62."

There is one epistle, among the canonical books of the New Testament, which is very generally ascribed to James the Less, the brother or cousin of Jesus, though some doubt has been entertained of its authenticity and apostolic authority, and no distinct reference to it is to be found in the writings of the earliest Fathers. In the time of Eusebius, however, it was universally received and read in the churches. It is a noble exhortation, full of good sense and spirit, dignified, independent, and explicit. Its value is of the highest description, both as it is an unreserved declaration of the intrinsic merit and importance of good works or virtue, and as it contains a most fearless, indignant, and forcible denunciation of the reigning vices and follies of the generation to whom the apostle wrote. A common opinion among the ancient writers of the Church is, that the first part of it was composed expressly to explain those passages of Paul's epistles which seem to slight good works, and make everything of faith, or mere belief; and that the severe rebukes and warnings which are contained in the latter portion of it were the chief occasion of the writer's being stoned to death by the Jewish populace; as that event is supposed to have taken place a short time after the publication of the epistle.

That the encomium of James on good works was intended to explain some of those things in Paul's writings which were hard to be understood is not improbable; but that it is in direct opposition to them, as some have thought, is not only improbable, but impossible. For it is impossible to read Paul's description of charity, in which he declares that it is greater than both faith and hope, and still to believe that he would so directly contradict himself as to reverse this order, and exalt faith above charity; or that he

intended by what he calls works, and the works of the law, what we mean by good works and Christian morality or virtue. The world have been too long, and much too vehemently disputing about the relative superiority of faith and works, and arraying James against Paul, and Paul against himself. It was, perhaps, a strong bias toward one side of this controversy, or rather a bigoted and dogmatical attachment to it, quite as much as any doubts of the genuineness and antiquity of James's epistle, which induced Luther to call it, in contempt, "an epistle of straw." *
Despite, however, of this coarse epithet of the Reformer, it has maintained its authority in the Christian Church, — an authority which, if intrinsic excellence and internal evidence have any weight, it amply deserves.

His day in the Calendar is May 1st, which is also dedicated to the Apostle Philip.

* "Epistola straminea," *a strawy epistle*, is the phrase applied by Luther to the epistle of James. The boldness, and perhaps even the rudeness, of the great Reformer qualified him to carry through his enterprise as he did, under circumstances and in an age which demanded not only decision, but a rough, uncompromising, unfeeling decision. Granting this to be the case, still he is not to be regarded as a pattern of Christian meekness, forbearance, or charity, — qualities which neither he, nor his contemporary Calvin, in any great degree possessed. Luther was more wild in his doctrine of faith than even Calvin; and he vented his spleen against good works on the excellent epistle of James, in an expression of contempt which would not be tolerated at the present day.

JUDE.

THE apostle who stands the tenth on Matthew's list, and is there called "Lebbeus whose surname was Thaddeus," is called in Mark's catalogue "Thaddeus," and in Luke's, "Judas the brother of James." We cannot fail to remark how carefully he is always distinguished from the other Judas. Matthew and Mark avoid naming him by the name which he held in common with the traitor; and Luke takes care to distinguish him by adding to that ill-omened appellation that he was the brother of James.

Jude, Judas, and Judah are one and the same name. Jude is merely an English abbreviation of Judas, and Judas is only a Greek pronunciation of the old Hebrew name of Judah. It means *the praise of the Lord.* Thaddeus is derived from the same root, and has a similar signification. Lebbeus appears to mean *a man of heart, or courage,* being derived from a word signifying *the heart.* These two last names were probably adopted to distinguish him from Judas Iscariot. All that is said of him in the sacred histories is, that at the last supper he asked Jesus why he was to manifest himself to his disciples, and not to the world. He was moved to put this question by the views which, in common with the other disciples, he entertained of the coming of the Messiah; who, as he thought, was to declare himself at last, with great pomp and external power. It was a mystery to him, therefore, how this victorious display was to be made to the small number of his disciples alone, and not to the whole admiring world. The answer of Jesus was not then, in all probability, understood. The meaning and substance of it was, that he and his Father would manifest themselves to those alone, and dwell in those alone, who loved him with that holy love, the fruits of which were righteousness and peace. This strong and beautiful declaration of the spirituality of the Messiah's kingdom is to be added to those which I have already noticed. The circumstance is related by John in the fourteenth chapter of his Gospel, who designates the apostle as "Judas, not Iscariot." No light is anywhere thrown upon his character; and all that we know of his condition is, that he was the brother of James the Less, and consequently a cousin of our Lord.

Other accounts of this apostle are so various and contradictory, that it would be wasting time to quote any of them. It is not known with certainty where he preached, or where he died, or whether he died a natural death, or suffered martyrdom. Most of the Latin writers say that he travelled into Persia, where his labors were very successful; but where, having irritated the Magi by reproving them for their superstitious practices, he was put to a violent death. Some of the Greeks affirm that he died quietly at Berytus; and the Armenians contend that in their country he was martyred.*

There is a passage from the ancient writer Hegesippus, as quoted by Eusebius, from which it appears that Jude was perhaps an husbandman before he was an apostle, and that he had descendants. The passage is thus given by Lardner: —

"When Domitian made inquiries after the posterity of David, some grandsons of Jude,

* It is in vain to endeavor to learn anything of this apostle from the writings of the Fathers, who, as is very evident from their contradictory stories, knew nothing about him. They generally preferred, however, to record the most groundless legend, rather than to confess their ignorance. "The men themselves," says Dr. Jortin, speaking of the Fathers, in his Remarks on Ecclesiastical History, "usually deserve much respect, and their writings are highly useful on several accounts; but it is better to defer too little than too much to their decisions, and to the authority of *antiquity*, that *handmaid to Scripture*, as she is called. She is like *Briareus*, and has *a hundred hands*, and these hands often clash, and beat one another."

called the Lord's brother, were brought before him. Being asked concerning their possessions and substance, they assured him that they had only so many acres of land, out of the improvement of which they both paid him tribute, and maintained themselves with their own hard labor. The truth of what they said was confirmed by the callousness of their hands. Being asked concerning Christ, and his kingdom, of what kind it was, and when it would appear, they answered, that it was not worldly and earthly, but heavenly and angelical; that it would be manifested at the end of the world, when, coming in great glory, he would judge the living and the dead, and render to every man according to his works. The men being mean, and their principles harmless, they were dismissed."

If the above passage be taken in connection with another from the old but doubtful book of the Apostolical Constitutions, in which the apostles are made to say, "Some of us are fishermen, others tent-makers, others husbandmen," the probability that Jude was a tiller of the soil is strengthened. At any rate, if the account of Hegesippus is to be relied on, he was married, and had descendants.

One epistle has been so generally ascribed to Judas, or Jude, that it has been admitted into the canon of the New Testament. There is

K

hardly another book, however, in that canon, which has been so much disputed. And yet there is no solid reason for rejecting the early tradition which gives it to this apostle. It was known in the first century, and there is no internal evidence against its apostolic origin. It was expressly quoted by Clement of Alexandria, who flourished about the year 194, and, after him, by succeeding Fathers. Lardner supposes it to have been written at some time between the years 64 and 66, that is, a few years before the destruction of Jerusalem.

October 28th is sacred, in the Western Calendar, to the memory of the Apostle Jude.

SIMON ZELOTES.

THE next apostle in order is another Simon, who, in the catalogues of Matthew and Mark, is surnamed "the Canaanite," and in that of Luke's Gospel, and the Book of Acts, "Zelotes." Some have thought that the surname, Canaanite, denoted the birthplace of the apostle; but others, with more probability, suppose that Canaanite is merely a Hebrew word, having the same signification with Zelotes, the Greek word used by Luke, and which means a zealot, or one who is extremely zealous. Simon may have received this appellation on account of his having once belonged to a sect or faction among the Jews who were called Zealots, or only on account of the warmth of his disposition, or the ardor with which he espoused and maintained the cause of Jesus.*

* "This word," says Cave, "has no relation to his country, or the place from whence he borrowed his original, as plainly descending from a Hebrew word which signifies *zeal*, and denotes a hot and sprightly temper. Therefore, what some of the Evangelists call *Canaanite*, others, rendering the Hebrew by the Greek word, style *Simon Zelotes*, or the *Zelot*."

It is probable, though not certain, that he is the same Simon who is mentioned as one of the brethren or cousins of our Lord. Of the history of his life nothing whatever is known; although the later writers and martyrologists of the Church pretend, as usual, to be intimately acquainted with it, and give us our choice of a sufficient number of contradictory legends. By some of them he is said to have labored in Egypt and Persia, and to have been martyred in the last-named country. By others, he is made to penetrate as far as Britain, and there to be crucified. "Nor could the coldness of the climate benumb his zeal," exclaims the honest Cave, "or hinder him from shipping himself and the Christian doctrine over to the western islands, yea, even to Britain itself. Here he preached, and wrought many miracles, and, after infinite troubles and difficulties which he underwent, suffered martyrdom for the faith of Christ, as is not only affirmed by Nicephorus and Dorotheus, but expressly owned in the Greek Menologies, where we are told that he went at last into Britain, and, having enlightened the minds of many with the doctrine of the Gospel, was crucified by the infidels, and buried there."

The two apostles, Simon and Jude, are commemorated on the same day, October 28th.

JUDAS ISCARIOT.

THE last, always the last, on the lists of the apostles, is Judas Iscariot. He is always branded, too, by those fearful and thrilling words, "who also betrayed him." And it is sad that we must close the roll which we have been examining of this glorious apostolic company with the name of a traitor.

His surname of Iscariot probably designates his birthplace; as it signifies "the man of Carioth or Kerioth," which was a town in the tribe of Judah. But this is hardly more than conjecture. There is a solemn obscurity hanging over the life of this man, shrouding everything in silent and immovable shadow, except one deed of gigantic enormity, which raises its high and desert head, and frowns in gloomy solitude over the surrounding waste of darkness and clouds. He is called the son of Simon. Who is Simon? Search the Scriptures for him. The search will be vain. He is only known, as has been forcibly said, — *only* known by the misfortune of having such a son.

The early dispositions of Judas must have been bad, or he would not have proved himself the wretch that he did, so soon after joining himself to such a Master; and a circumstance recorded in the Gospel of John plainly intimates to us what the chief vice of his character was. We are informed that on a visit which Jesus made to Bethany, where Lazarus lived, whom a little while before he had raised from the dead, a supper was made for him there; that Lazarus, with not one trace of death on his countenance, though but just now brought up from the grave, sat at table; and that Martha, with her usual assiduity, served. "Then took Mary a pound of ointment of spikenard, very costly, and anointed the feet of Jesus, and wiped his feet with her hair; and the house was filled with the odor of the ointment." This offering, though it may not have been useful, was certainly grateful and generous, and was beside in conformity with the custom of the country, and deserved, therefore, an approving comment from the friends and followers of Jesus. But what was the sequel? "Then saith one of his disciples, Judas Iscariot, Simon's son, who was to betray him, Why was not this ointment sold for three hundred pence, and given to the poor?" From an honest and really charitable man this remark would have been but a cold one, at such a season; but Judas was neither; and he said this, proceeds the historian, "not that he cared for the poor, but because he was a thief, and had the bag, and bare off what was put therein."* Thus it appears that the root of all this traitor's wickedness was avarice, and that it had already borne the deadly fruits of fraud and theft. He had the bag. He had been the treasurer of the fraternity; and so strong was his odious passion, and so weak was his principle, that he was unable to resist the temptation, which the trust afforded him, of purloining whatever he could from the common stock, which of necessity must have been a scanty one; and on this occasion he was grievously disappointed that he could not have the handling of the large sum of three hundred Roman denarii, under the pretence of distributing it to the poor. It is to be presumed that his peculiarities were not known to the apostles at that time, but that they came to light afterwards. If they had then been aware of his conduct, they would doubtless have spurned and avoided him.

Their Master, however, was acquainted both with what he did and with what he was; for it was on an occasion previous to this, that, in reminding the disciples of his own strong claims

---

* In our English Bible it is, "and bare what was put therein,"—a translation which does not seem to give the true meaning of the passage, though the Greek verb admits of both senses.

on their attachment, he said, "Have not I chosen you twelve? and one of you is a devil!" Here, too, as we are informed, "he spake of Judas Iscariot, the son of Simon." And let it be observed that neither the apostleship of Judas, nor his being the treasurer of the apostles, were causes of his avarice and treachery, and that therefore the knowledge which his Master possessed of his unsoundness is no excuse for it. If he had been a man of common goodness only, the trust which was reposed in him would have prompted him to a worthy exercise of it. Consequently it did not occasion, it only was the means of drawing forth and exposing, his baseness. Why our Saviour, acquainted as he was with the character of Judas, permitted him to hold the office of purse-bearer, or why he ever called him to be an apostle, are questions of a different import. Before we attempt to assign any reason or motive for the course of Jesus in this respect, let us attend for a moment to its consequences, and its bearing on the credibility of his Gospel.

I have already stated, in my introductory remarks, that, among the reasons which existed in the mind of our Lord for calling to himself a company of apostles, one probably was, that his conduct and instructions, being scrutinized by a number of individuals, and continually spread open to their observation, might be sufficiently attested and vindicated, at first to them, and afterwards to the world. This test was made more perfect by the introduction of one among his attendants whose heart was corrupt, and who would probably turn to as bad account as possible the confidence reposed in him. Thus we see that the inquisition to which the author of our religion was exposed was a complete one. The honest disciples would have published anything which they might have seen inconsistent with rectitude; and the traitor, the unprincipled disciple, would have magnified any fault or misconduct in his Master, if he could have found any there, as an excuse for his treachery. We ought not to be too hasty in ascribing motives to our Saviour in so grave a concern as this; but with the facts before us we cannot but feel satisfied that his character rests on a firmer basis, from having been thus laid open to the search of a wicked spy, and that his religion derives advantage from the scrutiny. And it is to be repeated, that the apostolic call did not make Judas a thief and a traitor; it found him one already; and if ever any man had the opportunity of reformation offered him, it certainly was he, who daily heard the instructions of Heaven, and beheld the example of perfection. We may conclude, therefore, that it was for the satisfaction of all future ages, for our conviction of the faultlessness of Jesus Christ, that Judas was made an apostle.

Commentators and harmonists disagree upon the question, whether the supper at Bethany was the same as that mentioned by Matthew as having been given in the house of Simon the leper. There are some circumstances common to both, and some peculiar to each. Macknight is confident that they were two distinct occurrences. A few of these arguments I will here repeat, which may lead the reader to further investigations.

"Although this supper (John xii. 2) is supposed by many to have been the same with that mentioned in Matt. xxvi. 6, upon examination they will appear to have been different. This happened in the house of Lazarus; that, in the house of Simon the leper. At this, Mary, the sister of Lazarus, anointed our Lord's feet, and wiped them with her hair; at that, a woman, not named, poured the ointment on his head. Here Judas only found fault with the action; there he was seconded by some of the rest. It seems all the disciples but Judas had let his first anointing pass without censure. But when they saw so expensive a compliment repeated, and that within a few days the one of the other, they joined with him in blaming the woman, and might think themselves warranted to do so, as they knew that their Master was not delighted with luxuries of any kind." Again he says: "The anointing after which Judas bargained with the priests happened only two days before the Passover, and consequently was different from that mentioned by John, which was six days before that solemnity."

"Thus it evidently appears," he proceeds, "that our Lord was anointed with spikenard three different times during the course of his ministry; once in the house of Simon the Pharisee, once in the house of Lazarus, and once in the house of Simon the leper. That this honor should have been done him so often needs not be thought strange; for in those countries it was common at entertainments to pour fragrant oils on the heads of such guests as they designed to distinguish with marks of extraordinary respect. The custom is alluded to, Psal. xlv. 7, 'God hath anointed thee with the oil of gladness above thy fellows.' Where this piece of civility was showed, it was an expression of the highest complacency, and produced great gladness in the person who was the object of it."

The answer of our Lord to the covetous remark of his disciple is narrated as follows: "Then said Jesus, Let her alone; against the day of my burial hath she kept this. For the poor always ye have with you; but me ye have not always." That is, "Suffer this woman to perform her pious work, and molest her not. She is anointing me for my burial; for I know that my hour is at hand, and that the grave is ready for me. Let her alone; it is the last testimony of her gratitude; it is the last mark of affection and reverence which I shall receive on earth; why then should it be called too costly? The claims of the poor are just and strong; I, surely, have never taught you to slight them; but the poor remain with you, and you will have abundant opportunity to relieve them; I am about to depart from you, and go to my Father."

This rebuke was a mild and touching one; but it affected not the stubborn heart of Judas; it even incited him, perhaps, to execute immediately his before-conceived purpose of betraying his Master into the hands of his enemies; for, very soon after it had been uttered, he went unto the chief priests, and bargained with them to deliver up Jesus into their power for thirty pieces of silver,—a sum not more than about a third of what the ointment had cost; and from that time he sought opportunity to betray him.

The value of the ointment was three hundred pence; the wages of treachery were thirty pieces of silver. The pence are supposed to be the Roman denarii, and a denarius is estimated at seven pence half-penny, English money; at which rate the whole cost of the ointment would be over nine pounds sterling. The pieces of silver were probably the Jewish shekels, each of which was of a weight equivalent to about two shillings and three pence; amounting in all to between three and four pounds. A different reckoning, however, has been adopted by some, as appears from the following passage from Jeremy Taylor's Life of Christ, which I quote at length, as containing other opinions on this subject. It will be perceived that the bishop takes it for granted that Mary Magdalen was the woman who anointed our Lord.

"It is not intimated, in this history of the life of Jesus, that Judas had any malice against the person of Christ; for when afterward he saw the matter was to end in the death of his Lord, he repented; but a base and unworthy spirit of covetousness possessed him; and the relics of indignation for missing the price of the ointment which the holy Magdalen had poured upon his feet burnt in his bowels with a secret, dark, melancholic fire, and made an eruption into an act which all the ages of the world could never parallel. They appointed him for hire thirty pieces; and some say that every piece did in value equal ten ordinary current deniers; and so Judas was satisfied by receiving the worth of the three hundred pence at which he valued the nard pistic. But hereafter let no Christian be ashamed to be despised and undervalued; for he will hardly meet so great a reproach as to have so disproportioned a price set upon his life as was upon the holy Jesus. St. Mary Magdalen thought it not good enough to aneal his sacred feet; Judas thought it a sufficient price for his head; for covetousness aims at base and low purchases, whilst holy love is great and comprehensive as the bosom of Heaven, and aims at nothing that is less than infinite."

It has been a subject of surprise with many commentators, that so small a bribe should have tempted Judas to commit so great a crime; and it does seem as if some other motive must have co-operated with the love of money, in bringing his mind to its dreadful determination. Among the solutions which have been proposed of this apparent enigma is the one which supposes that Judas was impatient of the delay of his Master to assume the state and magnificence of his Messiahship, and that his intention was to compel him to do so, by bringing him into such imminent peril, that he would be obliged to call his followers round him, work some signal miracle to free himself, and then mount the throne of David and of Israel. In this event, he of course calculated that he should come in for his share of those offices and rewards which he had been long pining for, and pining for in vain. Here, also, avarice is the governing motive; only on a much larger scale than in the action as it is simply narrated in the Scriptures.

There is something to say in favor of this explanation, and something too may be said against it. It is safest and easiest to take the bare Gospel statement, which merely informs us, that, for the consideration of thirty shekels of silver, Judas covenanted to betray his Master. No motive is expressly assigned for the act; but as he is represented as selfish and avaricious, we must presume that selfishness and avarice moved him to this last and most awful crime. With regard to the price of his treachery, a survey of human nature and human passions will not authorize us to say that any sum is too small to tempt habitual and absorbing avarice to any act or degree of wickedness. Earthly, sensual, and contemptible, there is no knowing how low this passion will creep, nor how high it will strike; how meanly it may dig for its dirty food, nor how daringly it may direct its poison.

Having concluded his bargain with the priests, and, as he thought, secretly, Judas resumed his place among the twelve, and the next that we hear of him is at the last supper.* As they were

---

* That is, the supper of the Passover. It has been disputed, whether Judas was or was not present when Jesus instituted his own supper, at the time of this feast; and it is a difficult point to

eating, Jesus said, "Verily I say unto you, that one of you shall betray me." At this intimation, the disciples, innocent as they all but one felt themselves to be, were exceedingly distressed, and they began each one to say unto him, "Lord, is it I?" Jesus, who had just before discovered the traitor, by a sign, to Simon Peter and John, answered, and said, "He that dippeth his hand with me in the dish, the same shall betray me. The Son of Man goeth, as it is written of him; but woe unto that man by whom the Son of Man is betrayed! it had been good for that man if he had not been born." Judas, who, in all probability, saw that his Master's hand and his own were together in the dish, and that he was consequently accused of the treason, but still, perhaps, relying on the secrecy with which he had made his bargain, thought that he now was obliged to say something; and pretending the same innocence as the rest, he asked the same question, "Lord, is it I?" And Jesus, using no more signs, but directly accusing the miserable culprit, answered, "Thou hast said." He then added, "That which thou doest, do quickly." Judas, finding that no disguise or equivocation would now serve him, went immediately out.

determine. "However it was," observes the author from whom I quoted last, "Christ, who was Lord of the sacraments, might dispense it as he pleased."

"And it was night," adds the historian. Night, indeed! How dark, how sad, how portentous! There never was another such since the world first woke from chaos. We seem to see it fall and settle like an outstretched pall, and embrace the whole of that devoted region with its mourning folds. Under its covering the wretched apostate — apostle no longer — stole forth to execute his purpose. What a night there must have been in his bosom and in his mind! And what a night, of doubt and fear and mournfulness, did he leave in the hearts of the eleven, who now listened sadly to their Master, as he pursued his melting, though calm, sustained, and heavenly discourse, and gave them his farewell exhortations and his farewell blessing!

It was yet night when the small company, now made smaller by desertion, having finished their supper and sung a hymn together, went out, as was the frequent custom of Jesus, to the Mount of Olives. Here he suffered his dreadful agony; and here Judas soon appeared, with an armed band, which he had received from the priests and Pharisees; for he knew that he should probably find his Master in this place of his usual resort. In order that his attendants might be sure of their victim, in this season of confusion and darkness, the traitor gave them a sign, telling them that whomsoever he should kiss, the same was he. Then going up to Jesus, as if he had been a friend, and intended to offer the common salutation of friendship and intimacy, he said, "Hail, Master!" and kissed him. Reproachfully Jesus said unto him, "Judas, betrayest thou the Son of Man with a kiss?" "Is it with a hypocritical kiss of affection and peace that you perform this deed of atrocious ingratitude?" Then Jesus said unto the chief priests, and captains of the temple, and the elders, who were come to him, "Be ye come out, as against a thief, with swords and staves! When I was daily with you in the temple, ye stretched forth no hands against me; but this is your hour, and the power of darkness." Then they took him, and brought him to the high-priest's house.

And now that Judas has accomplished his design, is he gratified? At first perhaps he was. But it was a momentary satisfaction. Reflection succeeded passion, and grief and remorse followed hard upon the footsteps of reflection. He could think now; and he could feel. He could think how good his Master had always been to him; how perfectly free from guilt or stain, and yet how condescending and pitiful to human error. He felt the baseness of his own conduct; he was appalled at the sight of his own enormous ingratitude; he began to hate himself, and to fear the light of morning, and to dread the aspect of that mild face, which, however mildly it might regard him, could speak nothing to his heart but judgment and agony. Morning came. The relentless and exulting enemies of Jesus met to adopt measures for securing their prey. As the fate of his Master approached nearer to its bloody catastrophe, the anguish of Judas became more intense, and his crime showed itself in all its horrors. Perhaps he did not apprehend that the priests would have pushed their malignity to the extreme of death. At any rate, his own malice and cupidity were wholly terrified away, and he resolved to make one wild effort to save the victim. He rushed to the conclave, with the now hateful silver grasped convulsively in his hand, and, reaching it out to his employers, he exclaimed, "I have sinned, in that I have betrayed innocent blood." Deluded man! Innocent or guilty, it was the same to them, so long as they could shed it. "And they said, What is that to us? See thou to that!" Stung to the quick by this cold and insulting reply, and feeling himself cast away like a tool which has been broken in the using, and having now no refuge from the fiends that were pursuing him, existence became a burden too heavy for him to bear; and he threw the pieces of silver on the pavement of the temple, "and departed, and went and hanged himself."

I know not how others may feel on perusing the history of this wretched man, but for my own part, I confess that my indignation is plentifully mingled with pity. How dark was the close of his short career! How terrible was the punishment of his guilt,—death by his own hands! The price of blood lies scattered at the feet of the priests; the betrayer has come to his end, even before the betrayed; his apostleship is ended; no softened multitude will listen to the tidings of salvation from his lips; no converts to a pure and purifying faith will bow to receive the waters of baptism from his hands; no countries will contend for the honor of his grave; no churches will call themselves by his name; no careful disciples compose his limbs; no enthusiastic devotees gather up his bones; his dust is scattered to the winds; his name is only preserved by its eternal ignominy. He was a martyr,—the first martyr,—but it was to avarice. He has had his followers too; but they have been only those, who, as wicked and as wretched as himself, have, from that day to this, and in the countless forms of selfishness, sold, for a few pieces of silver, their consciences, their Saviour, and their souls.*

---

* In the life of Thomas Firmin, that wealthy and eminently liberal and pious citizen and merchant of London in the seventeenth century, a curious legend is related from memory, respect-

By an observable coincidence, it so happened that the money which Judas had received and

ing the punishment of Judas in another state, which shows how the feelings of men relent, even towards the greatest transgressors. The legend is cited by the author, to illustrate the value of charitable deeds. As, notwithstanding its wildness, it is conceived and told in a truly poetical manner, and has, if I may judge, a favorable influence on the affections, I shall offer no apology for repeating it.

"I have read somewhere (but so long since, that I forget the author's name, and the subject of his book) that the punishment of Judas, who betrayed our Saviour, is, that he stands on the surface of a swelling, dreadful sea, with his feet somewhat below the water, as if he were about to sink. The writer saith, besides his continual horror and fear of going to the bottom, a most terrible tempest of hail and wind always beats on the traitor's naked body and head; he suffers as much by cold, and the smart of the impetuous hail, as it is possible to imagine he could suffer by the fire of purgatory, or of hell. But, saith my author further, in this so great distress Judas has one great comfort and relief; for, whereas the tempest would be insupportable if it beat always upon him from all sides, at a little distance from him and somewhat above him there is stretched out a sheet of strong, coarse linen cloth; which sheet intercepts a great part of the tempest. Judas regales himself by turning sometimes one side, sometimes another side, of his head and body to the shelter of this sheet. In short, the sheet is such a protection to him, that it defends him from the one half of his punishment. But by what meritorious action or actions did Judas deserve so great a favor? Our author answers, he gave just the same quantity of linen cloth to a certain poor family for shirting. It had been impossible that this gentleman should hit on such a conceit as this, but from our natural opinion of the value and merit of charity; it seems to us a virtue so excellent, that it may exclude even Judas from some part of his punishment. I can hardly afford to ask the reader's pardon for this tale; I incline to think, that divers others may be

returned became desecrated by his touch. There was a Jewish law which forbade that the price of blood should be put into the treasury. The priests, therefore, though they gathered up the pieces which the traitor had thrown down before them, were unable to appropriate them to the uses of the temple, and, after consulting together, agreed to purchase with them a field in the vicinity of Jerusalem, called the Potter's Field, to bury strangers in. The piece of ground thus purchased acquired the significant and fearful name of *The Field of Blood*.

When the tragedy of the crucifixion was over, and the eleven, comforted and reassured by the appearance of their risen Lord, had assembled together in Jerusalem, with the other disciples, to the number of about an hundred and twenty, Peter proposed to the company that a disciple should be chosen by lot to take "the ministry and apostleship, from which Judas, by transgression, fell." In the address which he made on this occasion, he gives an account of the death of Judas, which differs somewhat from the relation of Matthew. "Now this man," he says, "purchased a field with the reward of iniquity; and, falling headlong, he burst asunder in the

as well pleased with the wit of it, and the moral implied in it, as I have been, who remember it above forty years' reading, without remembering either the author or argument of the book."

midst, and all his bowels gushed out." Several explanations have been given to reconcile this discrepancy, either of which is sufficiently probable to answer the purpose. The most common one is, that Judas hung himself, as Matthew relates, and afterwards, by some accident, fell from the place where he was suspended, and was mangled in the shocking manner described by Peter.

According to the apostle's recommendation, his brethren proceeded to fill the traitor's forfeited place; and the lot fell upon Matthias, who had long been a disciple of Jesus, and is conjectured to have been one of the seventy. Thus was the miserable Judas, the apostate, the suicide, rejected from the apostolic company, even after his death, and his name and his memory blotted out, as entirely as was possible, from the records of the faithful. With the passages of the Scripture which were applied on this occasion by Peter, we will conclude his mournful biography. "For it is written in the Book of Psalms, Let his habitation be desolate, and let no man dwell therein; and, His bishopric let another take."

MATTHIAS.

For all the holy and spiritual purposes of apostleship, and for all the purposes of honorable remembrance in the Christian Church, the place of Judas Iscariot is vacated, as we have seen, and must be supplied by another, in order that the apostolic number may be complete. The name of Matthias must be joined to the foregoing list, though his name is not once mentioned in the Gospels. We shall then have thirteen names, but only twelve apostles still; twelve authorized founders of the Christian Church; twelve commissioned teachers of Christianity to the world; twelve judges of the twelve tribes of Israel.

The early determination of the eleven apostles to fill the spiritual throne from which Judas had fallen is proof of one or two interesting points. It proves, that, having recovered from their temporary panic, they were fully resolved to set about the work of their Master, and had no other idea but that of proclaiming his name, and planting his religion, according to his behest, and with the holy certainty of Divine assistance and protection, and of final success. It proves that their zeal and confidence were not confined within the limits of their own number, but were shared by many others, who stood ready to fill the vacant post of honor and danger, and to join in the cares and perils of the new and marvellous enterprise. It proves, moreover, the regard of the apostles for the integrity of the original number of their company; the number which the appointment of their Master had established and sanctified; the patriarchal number of twelve. Though two individuals were judged worthy of the forfeited station, only one could be received to it.

It was necessary that the candidates for the apostleship should be personally acquainted with the main events of the life of Jesus, in order that they might bear direct witness thereto. "Wherefore of these men," said Peter, in the assembly of one hundred and twenty disciples, "who have companied with us all the time that the Lord Jesus went in and out among us, beginning from the baptism of John, unto that same day that he was taken up from us, must one be ordained to be a witness with us of his resurrection." From this whole number, including very likely the seventy who are mentioned in the Gospels, two were selected as candidates, — "Joseph called Barnabas, whose surname was Justus, and Matthias"; and after prayer to God for the disposal of the lots, they were cast, "and the lot fell upon Matthias; and he was numbered with the eleven apostles."

All that we know of the apostle who thus closed up and made whole the sacred ring which had been so violently broken is related in the above account. We may say of Matthias, that he was one of those who had been interested from the beginning in the person and claims of Jesus, and had travelled from place to place with him and with his first twelve apostles, hearing his instructions, beholding his miracles, witnessing his holy life during his ministry on earth, and convinced by ocular demonstration of his resurrection from the dead. We may also be permitted to infer, from the selection which was made of him, that he was distinguished among the companions of the apostles and followers of Jesus for his mental and moral qualities, for his wisdom and his virtue.

Ecclesiastical history furnishes us with but poor and uncertain minutes of the apostolical labors of Matthias. An author of no great credit or antiquity asserts, "that he preached the Gospel in Macedonia; where the Gentiles, to make an experiment of his faith and integrity, gave him a poisonous and intoxicating potion, which he cheerfully drank off, in the name of Christ, without the least prejudice to himself; and, that when the same potion had deprived about two hundred and fifty of their sight, he, laying his hands upon them, restored them to their sight,—with a great deal more of the same stamp," says Cave, " which I have neither faith enough to believe, nor leisure enough to relate." Cave goes on to observe, that the more probable account of the apostle is, that from Judæa, where he first labored, he travelled eastward and preached in Cappadocia, where he at last received the crown of martyrdom on the cross.

Even the probability of this latter account is, however, but slight. Let it suffice, that he was a follower of our Lord from the first; that he was a companion of the apostles before he was chosen to be one of them; that he was considered worthy to be joined to their band; and that he must have labored for Christ and the Church in a manner conformable to the trust which was reposed in him, and the station which he was divinely allotted to fill.

The Greeks commemorate Matthias on the 9th of August, but the Western Churches on the 24th of February.

CONCLUDING REMARKS.

THE lives and characters of the twelve apostles of Christ have now been separately considered; but there are some general reflections upon them, regarded collectively, which naturally suggested themselves during the course that we have been through, and which may not prove uninteresting or uninstructive to those who have accompanied me in the way.

We find, with respect to the circumstances of their external condition, — their country, their fortunes, their education, — that they were such as most readily presented themselves to the search of Jesus, and yet not such, by any means, as we should suppose would have been effective in the accomplishment of his designs.

In the first place, the apostles were all Galileans, — natives or inhabitants of the district of Galilee. Seven of them, Peter and Andrew, James and John, Philip, Bartholomew, and Matthew, are expressly stated in the Gospels to have belonged to the district of Galilee. The same is in the highest degree probable of all the rest,

CONCLUDING REMARKS. 189

with the exception, perhaps, of Judas Iscariot. We find that the eleven, after Jesus had ascended into heaven before their sight, were thus spoken to by the two angels: "Ye men of Galilee, why stand ye gazing up into heaven?" And at the day of Pentecost, when they received the gift of tongues, the people who were present exclaimed, "Behold, are not all these who speak Galileans?" Indeed, so many of the first disciples of Christ were from Galilee, that they were all called Galileans at first, as we learn from contemporary historians.

This country constituted the northern portion of Palestine; and its people, though hardy and brave, were not much respected by the Jews of Jerusalem, who regarded them as illiterate and unpolished, and unworthy of producing a prophet. The Pharisees, reproving Nicodemus for the interest which he expressed in Jesus, said to him: "Art thou also of Galilee? Search, and look; for out of Galilee ariseth no prophet." The very speech of the Galileans was a provincial dialect, and betrayed their remoteness from the capital; as we have seen was the case with Peter in the palace of Caiaphas. In short they were looked down upon by the more cultivated, and, if I may use the epithet, *Attic* part of the nation, as a rude, unenlightened, Bœotian branch of the common Jewish family. Jesus, though born in Bethlehem, was brought up in Nazareth, which was the most despised town in this most despised province; and therefore, in selecting Galileans to be his apostles, he selected those who were nearest to him, and with whom he was most familiar. And yet what materials were they for constructing and building up a new religion, which was to be the wonder, the beauty and glory, of the earth! How little adapted they seem to be for their lofty destination! They are the last men, these poor Galileans, the very last men, as we should suppose, to confound the learned, to resist the mighty, to convert the world. They do not seem to be made for such a work. There is no fitness in them to be instructors and reformers. Their very birthplace forbids it. The choice of them, therefore, to be the intimate disciples of Christ, and the founders of a new religious system, appears to me to be a mark of the Divine mission of Christ, and the Divine character and origin of Christianity. To my ear the language of it is this: The person who, undertaking to introduce a peculiar and original faith to the world, selected, or, as it would rather appear, took almost carelessly up, his associates and confidential coadjutors, from his own neighborhood, from his own kindred, from the shores of a lake, from the streets of a village, from before his own door-stone, instead of seeking out the learned and the powerful from among the Pharisees and chief men of the nation, must have set out in his work with the assurance that there was a Power and a Wisdom above, which could and would supply every deficiency among his followers; and the event proved that the deficiency *was* supplied from a Divine, all-sufficient, and only sufficient Source.

These Galileans were also poor. Four of them were certainly fishermen; and others of their number were probably of the same profession. One was a publican, and of the inferior order of publicans.* They not only belonged to an undervalued province, but they were destitute of one of those means by which great ends are usually produced in the world. They were not, indeed, wretchedly destitute. They were above actual want, though they worked for their living; and their dwellings, though humble, appear to have been comfortable. But they were far from being rich; far from possessing any of that in-

* It is a habit among many of the Fathers and other writers on these subjects, to assert that Matthew was rich, in order to magnify the sacrifice which he made in leaving all to follow Jesus. But there is not the least ground in Scripture for supposing that he formed an exception to the general poverty, or at any rate very moderate circumstances, of the other apostles. He was able, to be sure, to give a supper, at which some Pharisees were present, who were not likely to honor with their presence the house of a poor man; but he might have done this and yet not have been very rich.

fluence and consequence which wealth so universally commands. And yet, without wealth, they effected what no wealth could have brought to pass, and became of more consequence than ever invests princes.

Besides these disadvantages, they were also unlearned. I do not mean that they were rudely ignorant, or that they were unacquainted with the sacred literature of their nation; but they were neither deeply versed in lore nor elegantly accomplished. They could not take a place among the well-educated portion of their countrymen. Their manner of expressing themselves at once betrayed this kind and degree of ignorance to those who were more polished and better instructed. Thus the council of elders and rulers before which Peter and John were arraigned perceived that those apostles were "unlearned and ignorant men." And yet they were not so unlearned and ignorant that they did not, both of them, give to the Church and to the world writings in the Greek language, which, though not exactly classical, were by no means despicable, even in their style. But their speech, provincial and uncultivated as it was, sent conviction to the hearts of multitudes; and their writings, simple and unpolished as they were, threw a new and heavenly radiance over that dark world, have instructed ages and generations, and impart more real knowledge on the highest objects of thought than the greatest philosophers of antiquity had ever been able to impart. To my mind this is a remarkable fact, and one which does not easily admit of but one explanation.

We may sum up the circumstances of the external condition of the apostles, by saying, that they were what would now be called plain, substantial men, in the lower walks of life. They were in a situation, not exceedingly depressed, and yet more remarkable for its humility than otherwise. Their education was only such a one as was usually bestowed on the common people of their nation, and in all probability consisted chiefly in a knowledge of the Scriptures of the Old Testament, which Scriptures they interpreted according to the instructions of the Rabbis, and the general expectations, opinions, and prejudices of their countrymen.

With regard to their natural dispositions, talents, and endowments of mind, there was among them the same assortment and variety of genius and character as would generally be found in the same number of men called together in a similar manner. Peter was irascible, impetuous, fervent, generous. John was amiable, affectionate, steadfast. Thomas was honest and scrutinizing. Matthew was modest and sensible. James the Greater was active and aspiring. James the Less was dignified in his sentiments and deportment. Some were forward, and some were retired. Some were eloquent, and others were silent. All but one appear to have been virtuous; and even that one was not without his use. They all, with that single exception, combined harmoniously in attachment to their Master and devotion to his cause. We may see in this fact, that Christianity was adapted to different dispositions, and received by different minds; that it was not merely the enthusiastic who accepted and supported it; that it was judged by different tests; that it was regarded through various optics; that zeal embraced it; that cool sense approved it; that candor and honesty were convinced by it; that even disappointed avarice could report nothing against it. We see too in this fact an instance of the truth, which is at once so obvious and so little regarded, that a variety of genius and disposition is in accordance with the designs of Providence in its most important operations with human instruments, as well as in the daily and social business of the world; and that a character is by no means to be despised because its qualities are not shining and striking. There are different parts to be performed, requiring different powers and capacities; and he who achieves his part, though it be a silent and undistinguished one, is a good servant.

CONCLUDING REMARKS. 195

We are told much, in the writings of the New Testament, of the words and actions of Simon Peter; but little or nothing of those of Simon Zelotes and Bartholomew; and yet these latter may have accomplished tasks which were necessary to the progress of the great work, but which would not have suited the peculiar capacity of Peter. They may have reached minds which he could not touch; they may have performed duties, subordinate indeed, but still necessary, such as he was not gifted to perform. Each apostle takes his own place, and stands easily and naturally in it; neither stretching after what was above, nor contemning what was below him. In this instance, as well as in others, we may derive a lesson from them.

In another point of view, the company of the apostles presents us with a spectacle which, though it may not be a very instructive, is certainly a pleasing one. Within their common fraternity there were no less than three distinct bands of natural brethren. Peter and Andrew were brothers; John and James the Greater were brothers; and so also were James the Less, Jude or Thaddeus, and Simon Zelotes. With the ties of a common faith, of a common toil, and a common danger, were thus beautifully blended the ties of consanguinity and domestic affection; and a texture of harmonious coloring was completed in this companionship, such as is seldom woven on earth. The three brethren last named were also near relations of Jesus himself. The reflections which are readily suggested by this circumstance are, that our Saviour was beloved at home as well as abroad; and that the familiarity of relationship did not impair the respect in which he was held as a master and teacher. We see also in this fact another cause of his love for his disciples, and of their love for him, — a cause which is far from diminishing our reverence for him, or our interest in them. They were not strangers to each other; they were not brought together merely by the attractions of sympathy, or the demands of a great work. They were not countrymen only; they were neighbors, partners, early acquaintances; they were more, for they were kinsmen, with the mutual attachments of kindred; and they go about on their labors before us, a more social, united, confidential, and interesting group, than if there had been no family bonds to strengthen and adorn their union.

Let us next view the apostles as authors, and as subjects of history. I should wonder at the state of that man's affections who could read the Gospels, two of which were written by apostles, without being struck by the exceeding modesty and self-forgetfulness of the disciples, and their absorbing attention to one individual, their venerated and beloved Master. There are no vaunts in those sacred histories; no instances of open or disguised egotism. When the writer speaks of his fellow-disciples, he relates with the utmost simplicity their faults, and prejudices, and want of faith, as well as the better parts of their characters. And he speaks of his Master, too, with equal simplicity, but with how much greater frequency and devotion! He brings every other person, every other thing, he brings himself, under perfect subordination to this main subject of his narrative. He does this, not artfully and intentionally, but unavoidably; from feeling, from impulse, from the conviction that there is but one individual of whom he is giving an account; and if others are mentioned, they are mentioned because they are in some manner connected with that person. If Jesus had occasion to praise one of his disciples, the evangelist records the fact without envy; if that disciple, or any other one is rebuked, he relates it without evasion or excuse. He keeps himself to the sayings and actions of his Master, as to his chief concern. He indulges in no inferences, no moral reflections, no expression of his own views or feelings; he writes pure history, simple narrative; and on all occasions he tells, without reserve and without suspicion, the plain truth; we see and feel that he does;

there is an honesty about every relation which cannot be mistaken or suspected. And we see and feel, too, that the chief personage of the history is not brought out into such entire relief, into such a concentration of light, by any effort or design on the part of the writer, but only and wholly on account of the unapproached sublimity and intrinsic superiority of the character itself.

There is one other circumstance in the lives of the apostles which I am bound to notice for the sake of its singularity and importance; and then I will leave them to the meditations and further inquiries of my readers. I have several times had occasion to speak of the national prejudices of these men, and the difficulty which they had to comprehend the entire spirituality of their Master's system and kingdom, and to admit into their associations with the Jewish Messiah and Saviour the ideas of poverty, lowliness, suffering, and death. Attached as they were to him by all the ties which we have enumerated, we see that when he was actually apprehended by his enemies, they all forsook him and fled; that they did not return to him; and that on the mount where he was crucified there was but one of them who appeared to witness the death of their Master and kinsman, and the extinction of all their hopes. The event was one for which they were wholly unprepared. It confounded them. Their preconceived opinions were so strong, that when Jesus had before spoken to them of his death, they shut up their ears and their eyes, they *would not* understand him. We do not find a single hint in the Gospels that they ever did understand him. The event itself was a blow which at once enlightened and convinced them, and scattered them abroad also, like sheep without a shepherd. This is one scene.

And now let us behold another, which immediately succeeds it. Not a great many days elapse when we find these very men, disheartened, disappointed, terrified, and dispersed as they had been, all gathered together again with one accord, fully recovered from all their depression, and with a settled resolution stamped on all their demeanor, which never marked them before, even while their Master was with them, to lead, combine, and encourage them. The catalogue of their names is full, with one vacancy only, which they immediately supply. They begin to preach the doctrines of a crucified Saviour, and we hear no more of their earthly notions of his kingdom. Their crude ideas and temporal hopes have, in a few days, vanished away. They preach Christianity, simply and purely. They gather to themselves thousands of converts. They are persecuted, imprisoned, threatened; they behold one of their number soon cut off with the sword; they are surrounded by enemies and temptations; and yet they never hesitate nor falter; no, not the weakest of them; there is not a single defection from their reunited brotherhood. They go through country after country, and toil after toil, laying down their lives, one after another, for the holy truth, and they leave disciples behind them everywhere, to teach, and dare, and suffer, and do, and die, as they did.

Now what is the cause of all this, and how is it to be accounted for? Unbelievers may have many explanations to give, and they may be ingenious ones. I have but one, and it is a simple one. It is, that their crucified Master rose from the dead as they have told us he did; that he instructed them as they have told us he did; and that the Holy Spirit, the Comforter, was sent from the Father, according to his promise, to enlighten and sustain them. In short, I consider the conduct of the apostles, at and after the death of Jesus, as perhaps the strongest proof of the reality of his glorious resurrection. If he rose from the dead and appeared to them, and instructed and confirmed them, I can account for the sudden change in their characters, and for their subsequent knowledge and perseverance and boldness and success. If he rose not from the dead, I cannot account for those things; and the whole subject remains to me a deep historical mystery.

Simple, honest, excellent men! raised up by Providence for wonderful ends by wonderful means! Your lives, unadorned as they are, and comprehended in a few plain words, are yet alone among the lives of men, — alone in the varieties and contrasts of their fortunes, alone in the multitude and importance of their consequences. We should be senseless if we did not perceive the influence which you have exerted on the character and opinions of mankind. We should be thankless if we did not acknowledge the benefits of that influence, and bless God that we live to know and feel them. And we humbly pray to God, the universal Father, the Source of all excellence and truth, that our fidelity to our common Master may be like yours; that our perseverance in executing his commands may be like yours; and that like yours may be our courage and constancy, if we should ever be called on to sacrifice comfort, worldly consideration, or life itself, to duty, conscience, and faith.

COLLECTS AND HYMNS.

SAINT ANDREW'S DAY.

November 30.

COLLECT. Almighty God, who didst give such grace unto thy holy Apostle Saint Andrew, that he readily obeyed the calling of thy Son Jesus Christ and followed him without delay; grant unto us all, that we, being called by thy holy word, may forthwith give up ourselves obediently to fulfil thy holy commandments, through the same Jesus Christ our Lord. *Amen.*

HYMN.

WHO leads the glorious company,
 The Apostles' sainted band?
First on the roll of duty see
 The holy ANDREW stand.

He first the promised Saviour sought
 Within his low abode;
And whom he found, to others taught,
 The Christ and Lamb of God.

And he, among the first, the call
   To tend his Lord obeyed;
Forsook his ship, his home, his all;
   And followed where he led.

" Fisher of men," by night, by day,
   His ready toils he set;
Intent to close his captive prey
   Within the Gospel net.

Nor scrupled he to yield his breath,
   By many a labor tried,
And die, with willing mind, the death
   By which his Master died.

And now his name with service meet,
   Leads on the sacred year,
And bids the Church prepare to greet
   The Saviour's Advent near.

BP. MANT.

SAINT THOMAS'S DAY.

December 21.

COLLECT. Almighty and everlasting God, who for the more confirmation of the faith didst suffer thy holy Apostle Thomas to be doubtful in thy Son's resurrection; grant us so perfectly, and without all doubt, to believe in thy Son Jesus Christ, that our faith in thy sight may never be reproved. Hear us, O Lord, through the same Jesus Christ, in whose name we ascribe unto thee all honor and glory, now and forevermore. *Amen.*

HYMN.

I HEAR the glorious Sufferer tell,
How on his cross he vanquished hell,
   And all the powers beneath;
Transported and inspired, my tongue
Attempts his triumphs in a song;
"How has the serpent lost his sting, and where's thy victory, death?"

But when he shows his hand and heart,
With those dear prints of dying smart,
   He sets my soul on fire;

Not the beloved John could rest
With more delight upon that breast,
Nor THOMAS pry into those wounds with more intense desire.

Kindly he opens me his ear,
And bids me pour my sorrow there,
  And tell him all my pains.
Thus while I ease my burdened heart,
In every woe he bears a part,
His arms embrace me, and his hand my drooping head sustains.

WATTS.

SAINT JOHN THE EVANGELIST'S DAY.

DECEMBER 27.

COLLECT. Merciful Lord, we beseech thee to cast thy bright beams of light upon thy Church, that it, being enlightened by the doctrine of thy blessed Apostle and Evangelist Saint John, may so walk in the light of thy truth, that it may at length attain to the light of everlasting life, through Jesus Christ our Lord. *Amen.*

HYMN.

AMONG the planets heavenly bright,
   Which round the Sun of glory shine;
No orb emits a purer light,
   A holier radiance, JOHN, than thine.

Apostle thou of Christ the Lord;
   Prophet of scenes to come decreed;
Historian of the incarnate Word;
   Martyr in will, if not in deed.

Yet by another name we deem
   Thy claim to high renown approved,
A name, of equal praise the theme,
   " Disciple, by thy Master loved."

Be ours to mark His portrait fair
  Whom thy recording pencil drew;
Be ours to mark thy faithful care,
  To his divine commandments true;

To note thy life; to see thee fling
  The beams of sacred truth abroad;
And soar with thee on eagle wing,
  And view unblamed the throne of God.

And may our faith, blest Saint, like thine
  By love to God and man be proved;
That we in some degree may shine,
  "Disciples by our Master loved."

Bp. Mant.

ANOTHER.

"Peter, seeing him, saith to Jesus, Lord, and what shall this man do? Jesus saith unto him, If I will that he tarry till I come, what is that to thee? follow thou me." John xxi. 21, 22.

"Lord, and what shall this man do?"—
  Ask'st thou, Christian, for thy friend?
If his love for Christ be true,
  Christ hath told thee of his end.
This is he whom God approves;
This is he whom Jesus loves.

Ask not of him more than this;
  Leave it in his Saviour's breast,
Whether, early called to bliss,
  He in youth shall find his rest,

Or armed in his station wait
Till his Lord be at the gate;—

Whether in his lonely course,
　(Lonely, not forlorn) he stay,
Or with love's supporting force
　Cheat the toil and cheer the way;
Leave it all in his high hand,
Who doth hearts as streams command.*

Gales from heaven, if so he will,
　Sweeter melodies can wake,
On the lonely mountain rill,
　Than the meeting waters make.
Who hath the Father and the Son
May be left,—but not alone.

Sick or healthful, slave or free,
　Wealthy, or despised and poor,—
What is that to him or thee,
　So his love to Christ endure?
When the shore is won at last,
Who will count the billows past?

Only, since our souls will shrink
　At the touch of natural grief,
When our earthly loved ones sink,
　Lend us, Lord, thy sure relief;
Patient hearts their pain to see,
And thy grace to follow thee.

　　　　　　　　　　KEBLE.

---

* "The king's heart is in the hand of the Lord as the rivers of water; he turneth it whithersoever he will." *Prov* xxi. 1.

SAINT MATTHIAS'S DAY.

FEBRUARY 24.

COLLECT. O Almighty God, who into the place of the traitor Judas didst choose thy faithful servant Matthias to be of the number of the twelve apostles; grant that thy Church, being always preserved from false apostles, may be ordered and guided by faithful and true pastors, through Jesus Christ our Lord. *Amen.*

HYMN.

WHO is God's chosen priest?
He who on Christ stands waiting day and night,
Who traced his holy steps, nor ever ceased,
    From Jordan banks to Bethphage height; —

Who hath learned lowliness
From his Lord's cradle, patience from his cross;
Whom poor men's eyes and hearts consent to bless;
    To whom, for Christ, the world is loss; —

Who both in agony
Hath seen him, and in glory ; and in both
Owned him divine, and yielded, nothing loath,
    Body and soul to live and die,

In witness of his Lord,
In humble following of his Saviour dear.
This is the man to wield the unearthly sword,
    Warring unharmed with sin and fear.

But who can e'er suffice—
What mortal—for this more than angel's task,
Winning or losing souls, thy life-blood's price?
    The gift were too divine to ask,

But thou hast made it sure
By thy dear promise to thy Church and Bride,
That thou, on earth, wouldst aye with her endure,
    Till earth to heaven be purified.
KEBLE.

A GOOD PRIEST.

GIVE me the priest these graces shall possess;—
Of an ambassador the just address;
A father's tenderness; a shepherd's care;
A leader's courage, which the cross can bear;
A ruler's awe; a watchman's wakeful eye;
A pilot's skill, the helm in storms to ply;
A fisher's patience; and a laborer's toil;
A guide's dexterity to disembroil;
A prophet's inspiration from above;
A teacher's knowledge,—and a Saviour's love.
BP. KENN.

SAINT PHILIP AND SAINT JAMES'S* DAY.

May 1.

COLLECT. O Almighty God, whom truly to know is everlasting life; grant us perfectly to know thy Son Jesus Christ to be the way, the truth, and the life, that following the steps of thy holy Apostles Saint Philip and Saint James, we may steadfastly walk in the way that leadeth to eternal life, through the same thy Son Jesus Christ our Lord. *Amen.*

HYMN.

HOLY Jesus, Saviour blest
As, by passion strong possest,
Through this world of sin we stray,
Thou to guide us art the WAY.

Holy Jesus, when the night
Of error blinds our clouded sight,
Round the cheering day to throw,
Saviour, then the TRUTH art thou.

Holy Jesus, when our power
Fails us in temptation's hour,

* James the Less.

All unequal to the strife ;
Thou to aid us art the LIFE.

Who would reach his heavenly home;
Who would to the Father come ;
Who the Father's presence see ;
Jesus, he must come by thee.

BP. MANT

SAINT JOHN THE BAPTIST'S DAY.

June 24.

COLLECT. Almighty God, by whose providence thy servant John Baptist was wonderfully born, and sent to prepare the way of thy Son, our Saviour, by preaching repentance; make us so to follow his doctrine and holy life, that we may truly repent according to his preaching; and, after his example, constantly speak the truth, boldly rebuke vice, and patiently suffer for the truth's sake; through Jesus Christ our Lord. *Amen.*

HYMN.

HARK through the lonely waste,
By foot of man unpaced,
"Prepare the way," a warning voice resounds!
"Level the opposing hill,
The hollow valley fill,
Make straight the crooked, smooth the rugged grounds;
Prepare a passage,— form it plain and broad;
And through the desert make a highway for our God!"

Thine, BAPTIST, was the cry,
In ages long gone by,

Heard in clear accents by the prophet's ear;
    As if 't were thine to wait,
    And with imperial state
Herald some Eastern monarch's proud career;
Who thus might march his host in full array,
And speed through trackless wilds his unresisted way.

    But other task hadst thou
    Than lofty hills to bow,
Make straight the crooked, the rough places plain.
    Thine was the harder part
    To smooth the human heart,
The wilderness where sin had fixed his reign;
To make deceit his mazy wiles forego,
Bring down high-vaulting pride, and lay ambition low.

    Such, Baptist, was thy care,
    That no obstruction there
Might check the progress of the King of kings;
    But that a clear highway
    Might welcome the array
Of heavenly graces which his presence brings;
And where repentance had prepared the road,
There faith might enter in, and love to man and God.
                             Bp. Mant.

SAINT PETER'S DAY.

June 29.

COLLECT. O Almighty God, who by thy Son Jesus Christ didst give to thy Apostle Saint Peter many excellent gifts, and commandedst him earnestly to feed thy flock; make, we beseech thee, all pastors diligently to preach thy holy word, and the people obediently to follow the same, that they may receive the crown of everlasting glory, through Jesus Christ our Lord. *Amen.*

HYMN.

LORD! when thy PETER, weak in faith,
 By terror too severely tried,
Failed in thine hour of threatened death,
 And thee forsook, and thee denied;—

When thrice his ear the challenge heard,
 And thrice his tongue renounced thy name,
And each sad time the recreant word
 More loud and more impassioned came;—

One look from thee his fault reproved,
 And made his slumbering conscience start;
One look from thee, so dearly loved,
 Spoke daggers to his bleeding heart;

And sent him forth a prey to grief,
  Unheeded all his former fears,
To seek in solitude relief
  From bitter and repentant tears.

Lord! when by human frailty led,
  We pass thy gracious warning by,
Prone as we are awry to tread,
  And thee forsake, and thee deny; —

Grant us to feel the keen rebuke,
  By conscience, faithful guardian, sent,
As if we saw thy pitying look,
  When on thy frail Apostle bent.

That pitying look! O may it melt
  Our hearts in penitential showers!
May Peter's grief by us be felt,
  And O, be his forgiveness ours!

Bp. Mant.

ANOTHER.

"When Herod would have brought him out, the same night Peter was sleeping." *Acts* xii. 6.

Thou thrice denied, yet thrice beloved,
  Watch by thine own forgiven friend;
In sharpest perils faithful proved,
  Let his soul love thee to the end.

The prayer is heard, — else why so deep
  His slumber on the eve of death?
And wherefore smiles he in his sleep
  As one who drew celestial breath?

He loves and is beloved again, —
   Can his soul choose but be at rest?
Sorrow hath fled away, and Pain
   Dares not invade the guarded nest.

He dearly loves and not alone:
   For his winged thoughts are soaring high
Where never yet frail heart was known
   To breathe in vain affection's sigh.

He loves and weeps, — but more than tears
   Have sealed thy welcome and his love, —
One look lives in him, and endears
   Crosses and wrongs where'er he rove:

That gracious chiding look, thy call
   To win him to himself and thee,
Sweetening the sorrow of his fall,
   Which else were rued too bitterly.

Even through the veil of sleep it shines,
   The memory of that kindly glance; —
The Angel watching by divines
   And spares awhile his blissful trance.

Or haply to his native lake
   His vision wafts him back, to talk
With JESUS, ere his flight he take,
   As in that solemn evening walk,

When to the bosom of his friend,
   The Shepherd, he whose name is Good,
Did his dear lambs and sheep commend,
   Both bought and nourished with his blood:

Then laid on him the inverted tree,
   Which, firm embraced with heart and arm,
Might cast o'er hope and memory,
   O'er life and death, its awful charm.

With brightening heart he bears it on,
   His passport through the eternal gates,
To his sweet home, — so nearly won,
   He seems, as by the door he waits,

The unexpressive notes to hear
   Of angel song and angel motion,
Rising and falling on the ear
   Like waves in Joy's unbounded ocean.

His dream is changed, — the Tyrant's voice
   Calls to that last of glorious deeds, —
But as he rises to rejoice,
   Not Herod but an Angel leads.

He dreams he sees a lamp flash bright,
   Glancing around his prison room, —
But 't is a gleam of heavenly light
   That fills up all the ample gloom.

The flame that in a few short years
   Deep through the chambers of the dead
Shall pierce, and dry the fount of tears,
   Is waving o'er his dungeon-bed.

Touched he upstarts, — his chains unbind, —
   Through darksome vault, up massy stair,
His dizzy, doubting footsteps wind
   To freedom and cool moonlight air.

Then all himself, all joy and calm,
  Though for a while his hand forego,
Just as it touched, the martyr's palm,
  He turns him to his task below;

The pastoral staff, the keys of heaven,
  To wield awhile in gray-haired might,
Then from his cross to spring forgiven,
  And follow JESUS out of sight.
KEBLE.

SAINT JAMES'S* DAY.

July 26.

COLLECT. Grant, O merciful God, that as thine holy Apostle Saint James, leaving his father and all that he had, without delay was obedient unto the calling of thy Son Jesus Christ, and followed him; so we, forsaking all worldly and carnal affections, may be evermore ready to follow thy holy commandments, through Jesus Christ our Lord. *Amen.*

HYMN.

AND couldst thou, JAMES, to win the meed
Of glory for his saints decreed,
   Thy Saviour's cup of sorrow taste?
And couldst thou bear above thee spread
The waves baptismal, dark and dread,
   Which o'er thy Saviour past?

Thou couldst: such aid his Spirit lent!
The stripes, the bonds, the imprisonment,
   The scornful look, the taunting word,
The angry council's stern decree,
The tyrant's rage and cruelty,
   And last the fatal sword:

* The Greater.

These came in turn; and then thy death!
O thou, to wear a martyr's wreath
　The first of all thy brotherhood!
First of thy Saviour's chosen train,
Like him the cup of woe to drain,
　Like him baptized in blood!

We dare not rend the veil aside
By which the All-knowing wills to hide
　The secrets of the unseen world;
But to our vision it should seem,
Might we without irreverence deem
　Of that dark veil unfurled;

Should seem that thou wert there to see,
O James, O son of Zebedee,
　And he, the favored of your Lord,
Martyr with thee at least in will;
Together throned on God's high hill
　Beside your King adored.

For not in vain his word was given
That ye who have through sufferings striven,
　For him and for his Gospel known,
With him shall in his glory dwell,
And judge the tribes of Israel,
　Throned by Messiah's throne.

Nor vain the word, that whosoe'er
Shall the Messiah's name prefer
　To houses, parents, children, wife,
Shall hundred-fold by him be blest,
Be welcomed to his Father's rest,
　And dwell in endless life.

Bp. Mant.

SAINT BARTHOLOMEW'S DAY.

August 24.

COLLECT. O Almighty and everlasting God, who didst give to thine Apostle Bartholomew grace truly to believe and to preach thy word; grant, we beseech thee, unto thy Church to love that word which he believed, and both to preach and receive the same, through Jesus Christ our Lord. *Amen.*

HYMN.

" BEHOLD, in whom no guile I find,
   An Israelite indeed ! "
NATHANAEL, thus thy virtuous mind
   Did Israel's sovereign read.

A guileless heart! what fairer scene
   In all this world below
Does nature's loveliness contain,
   Or God's creation show ?

Fair are the snow-wreaths that infold
   Yon Alpine mountain's head;
Fair is the stream, all crystal, rolled
   Clear o'er its pebbly bed;

Fair is the star of evening bright,
    A gem in heaven's blue zone;
And fair the moonlight's robe of white
    O'er earth's green surface thrown;

But Alpine snow, nor crystal stream,
    Can pure delight impart,
Nor moon, nor evening planet's gleam,
    To match the guileless heart.

For these material works of God
    Of him memorials stand,
And tell the Maker's power abroad,
    The wonders of his *hand:*

But guileless truth and innocence,
    By God to men consigned,
Reflect his moral excellence,
    And image of his *mind.*

                              BP. MANT.

SAINT MATTHEW'S DAY.

SEPTEMBER 21.

COLLECT. O Almighty God, who by thy blessed Son didst call Matthew from the receipt of custom, to be an apostle and evangelist; grant us grace to forsake all covetous desires, and inordinate love of riches, and to follow the same thy Son Jesus Christ our Lord, who liveth and reigneth with thee, world without end. *Amen.*

HYMN.

PREPARE the feast! the viands bring,
   Heap high the festal board!
The subject welcomes Israel's king;
   The follower greets his Lord.

But who is he, the host, whose care
   Provides the costly feast?
And who are they assembled there
   Around the heavenly guest?

'T is MATTHEW, 't is the publican;
   The favored host is he
Who sat, a much-despised man,
   Beside Tiberias' sea.

And they, the guests assembled round,
    They boast no better name;
One in disgraceful union found,
    Allied to sin and shame.

O holy Jesus, and are these
    Associates meet for thee?
Is this the host thy soul to please,
    And this the company?

"Not to the righteous was I sent;
    Not to the whole I cry;
I call the sinner to repent;
    The sick man's health am I.

" For them my glory I resigned;
    For them endure the grave;
I came the wandering sheep to find,
    The perishing to save."

Shepherd of Israel, Saviour dear!
    Whose voice thy duteous sheep
Safe in thy fold delighted hear,
    And to thy pasture keep;

Repentant, lo! to thee we turn,
    To thee for health we pray;
Give us what thou reveal'st to learn,
    And what thou bidd'st obey.

                      Bp. Mant.

ANOTHER.

Ye hermits blest, ye holy maids,
   The nearest heaven on earth,
Who talk with God in shadowy glades,
   Free from rude care and mirth;
To whom some viewless teacher brings
The secret lore of rural things,
The moral of each fleeting cloud and gale,
The whispers from above, that haunt the twilight vale; —

Say, when in pity ye have gazed
   On the wreathed smoke afar,
That o'er some town, like mist upraised,
   Hung, hiding sun and star,
Then as you turned your weary eye
To the green earth and open sky,
Were ye not fain to doubt how Faith could dwell
Amid that dreary glare, in this world's citadel?

But Love's a flower that will not die
   For lack of leafy screen,
And Christian Hope can cheer the eye
   That ne'er saw vernal green.
Then be sure that Love can bless
Even in this crowded wilderness,
Where ever-moving myriads seem to say,
Go — thou art naught to us, nor we to thee — away!

There are in this loud stirring tide
   Of human care and crime,
With whom the melodies abide
   Of the everlasting chime;

Who carry music in their heart
Through dusky lane and wrangling mart,
Plying their daily task with busier feet
Because their secret souls a holy strain repeat.

How sweet to them, in such brief rest
　　As thronging cares afford,
In thought to wander fancy-blest,
　　To where their gracious Lord,
In vain, to win proud Pharisees,
Spake, and was heard by fell disease, —
But not in vain, beside yon breezy lake,
Bade the meek PUBLICAN his gainful seat forsake.

At once he rose, and left his gold;
　　His treasure and his heart
Transferred, where he shall safe behold
　　Earth and her idols part;
While he beside his endless store
Shall sit, and floods unceasing pour
Of Christ's true riches o'er all time and space,
First angel of his Church, first steward of his grace.

Nor can ye not delight to think
　　Where he vouchsafed to eat,
How the pure Master did not shrink
　　From touch of sinner's meat;
What worldly hearts and hearts impure
Went with him through the rich man's door;
That we might learn of him lost souls to love,
And view his least and worst with hope to meet above.

These gracious lines shed Gospel light
　　On Mammon's gloomiest cells,

As on some city's cheerless night
    The tide of sunrise swells,
Till tower, and dome, and bridge-way proud
    Are mantled with a golden cloud,
And to wise hearts this certain hope is given,
" No mist that man may raise shall hide the eye of Heaven."

    And oh! if even on Babel shine
        Such gleams of Paradise,
    Should not their peace be peace divine,
        Who day by day arise
    To look on clearer heavens and scan
    The work of God untouched by man?
Shame on us who about us Babel bear,
And live in Paradise, as if God was not there!

                                                       KEBLE.

SAINT SIMON AND SAINT JUDE'S DAY.

October 28.

COLLECT. O Almighty God, who hast built thy Church upon the foundation of the apostles and prophets, Jesus Christ himself being the head corner-stone, grant us so to be joined together in unity of spirit by their doctrine, that we may be made a holy temple acceptable unto thee, through Jesus Christ our Lord. *Amen.*

HYMN.

As at the first, by two and two
   His herald saints the Saviour sent
To soften hearts like morning dew,
   Where he to shine in mercy meant;

So evermore he deems his name
   Best honored and his way prepared,
When watching by his altar-flame
   He sees his servants duly paired.

He loves when age and youth are met,
   Fervent old age and youth serene,
Their high and low in concord set
   For sacred song, joy's golden mean.

He loves when some clear soaring mind
   Is drawn by mutual piety
To simple souls and unrefined,
   Who in life's shadiest covert lie.

Or if perchance a saddened heart
   That once was gay and felt the spring,
Cons slowly o'er its altered part,
   In sorrow and remorse to sing,

Thy gracious care will send that way
   Some spirit full of glee, yet taught
To bear the sight of dull decay,
   And nurse it with all pitying thought;

Cheerful as soaring lark, and mild
   As evening blackbird's full-toned lay,
When the relenting sun has smiled
   Bright through a whole December day.

These are the tones to brace and cheer
   The lonely watcher of the fold,
When nights are dark, and foemen near,
   When visions fade and hearts grow cold.

How timely then a comrade's song
   Comes floating on the mountain air,
And bids thee yet be bold and strong,—
   Fancy may die, but Faith is there.

                              KEBLE.

ANOTHER.

FATHER, gracious Father, hear
Faith's effectual fervent prayer;
Hear, and our petitions seal,
Let us now the answer feel.
Still our fellowship increase;
Knit us in the bond of peace;
Join our new-born spirits, join
Each to each, and all to thine.

Build us in one body up,
Called in one high calling's hope;
One the Spirit whom we claim,
One the pure baptismal flame,
One the faith, and common Lord,
One the Father lives adored,
Over, through, and in us all,
God incomprehensible.
WESLEY.

THE END.

Cambridge : Stereotyped and Printed by Welch, Bigelow, & Co.

www.ingramcontent.com/pod-product-compliance
Lightning Source LLC
Chambersburg PA
CBHW031746230426
43669CB00007B/501